Communication and
Communication Barriers
in Sociology

Communication and Communication Barriers in Sociology

Gunnar Boalt, Herman Lantz,
Torgny Segerstedt, Paul Lindblom,
Charles Snyder et al.

ALMQVIST & WIKSELL INTERNATIONAL
Stockholm/Sweden

A Halsted Press Book
JOHN WILEY & SONS
New York · London · Sydney · Toronto

© 1976 Almqvist & Wiksell International, Stockholm
ISBN 91 22 00037-2

Published in the U.S.A., Canada and Latin America by Halsted Press,
a Division of John Wiley & Sons Inc., New York

Library of Congress Cataloging in Publication Data
Main entry under title:

Communication and communication barriers in sociology.
1. Sociology–Study and teaching–Addresses, essays, lectures.
2. Sociological research–Addresses, essays, lectures.
3. Sociologists–United States–Addresses, essays, lectures.
I. Boalt, Gunnar.
HM45.C64 1976   301'.07'2   75-44623
ISBN 0-470-15016-5

Printed in Sweden by
Almqvist & Wiksell, Uppsala 1976

Contents

Chapter 1

Introduction to the problem of university and research

Herman R Lantz

This book is concerned with the development and role of research in sociology departments within the university. It undertakes an examination of this process, and related processes, primarily in Sweden, but also in the United States. It is difficult to discuss the development of research without taking into account the larger social context in which educational processes unfold. Hence, we shall deal with some rather broad ranging views with a specific focus on various internal factors within universities, themselves. Hopefully the material which follows has implications for different academic departments in many settings, but whether this is so is still to be determined. At the outset we wish to take a global view of universities both in Europe and America.

The basic premise of this presentation is that there have been a number of factors which have worked against the development of research careers in sociology. We do not dispute the value of other rules, nor the fact that research can be meaningless, ritualistic and without lasting value. But we do assert that the development of sociology is dependent on the development of research and research careers. We hope, in this section, to analyze several factors which have interfered with the development of research.

A first difference between universities in Sweden and America has to do with the role and position of research. In Sweden the university in many respects was considered the center for research, and the faculty/member's major responsibility was to contribute to the body of research in his field. It was the student's major responsibility to derive what he could from his professor. We recognize to be sure that universities in Sweden in recent years have been under public pressure, and under pressure from students, to place more emphasis on teaching-service. The extent of long range change is difficult to determine, however. American universities have not been nearly so committed to a research orientation, and few universities in America today would be prepared to state that the pursuit of research and publication was their major aim. In the United States many universities have been unclear as to the role of research, especially sociological research. This is especially the case for pure research, since applied research, given the pragmatism of American higher education, has held high priority. This statement can be made in spite of the general expansion of research in the 1950's and 1960's, an expansion due primarily to massive state and federal funding. Nevertheless, the vast majority of sociologists were not involved in research (Gross and Grambsch, 1968: 87–89; Nisbet, 1971: 71–87). Most universities in America assert that they are devoted to *teaching, service and research* (Gross and Grambsch, 1968: Ch. 3.). Such ambivalence in the U.S. about research was accentuated by the number of teacher training schools which existed in large numbers until the 1950's. Almost all of these teacher training institutions became universities in overall structure. They developed a wide variety of undergraduate and graduate colleges, yet in several essential ways the philosophy of the teachers college remained. They held, and in some instances continue to hold, to higher teaching loads for faculty, they continue to stress service to the community while research becomes secondary. The inability to shift perspective from a teachers college to a university is to be found in both the faculty and administration of these institutions (Gaston, 1973). Many of the faculty, having spent years in a teacher training context, find it difficult to reorient their career pattern. Many administrators at these institutions are drawn from the same ranks, and find it difficult to demand of others what they have been unable to do themselves. Taking American universities as a whole, one notes that not all segments of the university are equally ambivalent about the development of research, nor is the ambivalence the same at different stages in the development of a university. Ambivalence appears to be greatest during the transitional stages of university development. It is less at the stage of underdevelopment, and ambivalence is less when the university is developed. The teacher training institution was not ambivalent about research. These institutions did not expect research and often discouraged any research, since it was believed that research detracted from teaching. Similarly a highly developed institution has already made a commitment to research, and its policies are reflected in this commitment. It is the university in a state in transition with conflicting perspectives that remains the most ambivalent, and such universities are plentiful in the United States (Gross and Grambsch, 1968: Ch. 2). With regard to the administrative structure within a developing university there are degrees of ambivalence, ranging from the chairman who is probably the most ambivalent. The president and his staff, often the leaders in change from a teacher oriented to a research oriented institution, have little changing to do with respect to their own roles. In other respects, however, the development of research in a university represents special problems from the administrative point of view. The research productivity of a faculty can raise the prestige and stature of a university. On the other hand, researchers are often difficult to deal with. Research scholars make more demands, are more difficult to control, and pose a threat to the administration since their very productivity enables them to seek and find other positions (Nisbet, 1971: 88–100). These potential difficulties, however, are more likely to be experienced at the lower administrative levels of dean or chairman (Gross and Grambsch, 1968: 88–90). Thus, it is not surprising to find that as one goes down into the structure and moves closer to the faculty, administrative ambivalence toward research may increase. Perhaps the most important variable which may explain such ambivalence to change on the part of those in administrative roles has to do with the impact of change on relationships with the faculty. A shift in orientation from an institution which has emphasized teaching to one which emphasizes research and publications represents a basic and drastic shift in career orientation for the average faculty member. For those who have not been involved in research the shift can be extremely threatening. The result may be anxieties of serious proportions. The dean interprets the administrative view regarding research. The security of his role depends in part on his chairmen, who may rebel and refuse to support him on research policies, and they may also refuse to support him on other issues as well. On the other hand, by rejecting an administrative decision regarding an orientation toward research, he can alienate those above him. There are other complications for the dean. Political support and allegiance are always greatest when the criteria for such support are broadly based. Thus, in a purely political sense, a political figure is better off if he can appeal to all religious groups rather than one. The same applies to the university administrator, particularly the dean of a college. There is value in not basing the reward system on a single criterion such as research, but on several criteria—teaching, service, loyalty, longevity—since it then becomes possible to reward many more people (Nisbet, 1971: 127–131). Under these circumstances the university administrator has "something for everyone". In addition the greater the basis for reward the greater the opportunity to manipulate the reward system in different ways. If a dean chooses he can elevate outstanding service, or teaching, or research to justify how and why different faculty have been rewarded. A major problem confronting a dean is that probably only a relatively small number of his faculty are capable of engaging in research and publication. Hence, the more he rewards this small segment, the more likely he is to alienate large numbers of the faculty. All of these factors create obstacles to the development of a consistent policy toward research.

The chairman, who is closest to the faculty, occupies the most sensitive position. He is subject to many of the problems we have just described (Gross and Grambsch, 1968: 92–94). If he imposes a research orientation on his faculty against their wishes, he may fail to get their support in the future. If the chairman fails to support the administration, he loses administrative support. Moreover, as the chairman imposes norms of research and publication on his faculty, his faculty often have similar expectations for him. This results in additional burdens for the chairman.

The burdens of the office of chairman in academic departments in the United States are so great as to require the virtual abandonment of a scholarly career. For a chairman is at best very vulnerable. For as one's scholarly career disappears, security in one's role becomes increasingly based on a capacity to satisfy a faculty with many interests, not only those with research interests. If the chairman wishes to remain in his role, it may also require a capacity to compromise on the importance of research so as not to offend non-research constituencies within a department.

In general, administrators with scholarly backgrounds are less likely, on the average, to be ambivalent about research, than are those without such backgrounds (Gaston, 1973). In this respect European and American universities differ in where they draw administrators from. In Europe these are much more likely to come from people who have an established record of academic accomplishment. In the United States administrators may have earned scholarly reputations, but, more likely, they are persons who have often left a scholarly career in search of an administrative career.

A second difference between universities in Sweden and America is one of orientation. In Sweden one finds more of an elitist concept, involving higher education for the intellectually capable who come from upper income backgrounds, than is the case in America. While it is a fact that Swedish universities have moved to a more egalitarian notion of education, the move is a relatively recent one. In America the move toward egalitarian notions involving the education of masses of people emerged in the latter part of the 19th century, and became much more pronounced following World War II. This movement of large numbers of students became significant in developments following the end of World War II.

A third difference between universities in Sweden and the United States is the impact of World War II. The drain of youth for the armed forces in the United States resulted in a serious interruption of many careers and a pent up demand for education at the end of the war. Higher education in the United States, following World War II, faced enormous demands for faculty; demands possibly unknown at any time in the history of higher education. These demands continued into the 1960's. One major effect was that students were encouraged to undertake graduate study in sociology who were often lacking in motivation, commitment and competence for research. Certainly it is true that in the post World War II period there were some excellent research centers, and many students were competently trained and motivated, but it is clear that this only applies to a relatively small number of students trained in the period following the end of World War II.

Many Doctoral students came in large numbers from the middle and lower middle classes; they were interested primarily in college teaching as a vocation. Academic life represented a move up, economically and socially. Moreover, insofar as there was a serious commitment to sociology, it stemmed from a desire for social change and reform; a social reform based on lectures and education rather than a belief in the value of research. It had a muck-raking, reformistic ideology of investigating and revealing conditions, but not studying them in any systematic way.

Graduate programs, often had many deficiencies, including large graduate classes and an overworked faculty. Moreover, graduate faculty, themselves, in the United States were not, and have not been, altogether consistent or clear as to the meaning of the Ph.D. Certainly for many it has not necessarily been a research degree, but was instead simply a hurdle to be surmounted before a candidate could qualify for a position. Indeed, it has not been uncommon for a dissertation committee to pass a weak candidate because they believed that given the candidate's lack of ability and given the position he would hold at college X, it would not be necessary to have research competence. Such graduates with masters and Ph.D. degrees, were sent out in large numbers to occupy positions in various colleges and universities in the post World War II period. The consequences have been several. First, the necessary models and the appropriate socialization for a career in science often were not developed. Textbooks dealing with methodology were unintentionally misleading and portrayed a mechanistic image of how ideas emerge and how scientific work is conducted. The commitment to research was peripheral, and when the realities of producing research became apparent, there was often a rejection of, and disinterest in, research. Without a basic interest in research, there was never a real appreciation for the accumulation of data and the systematic study of a problem. It was the dramatic answer to a special problem that had much more appeal than systematic study. The concern for painstaking efforts in building knowledge was not well established. Probably the effect of many of these post World War II students on the development of research programs in sociology was essentially negative. In the post World War II period the expansion in higher education was also uneven, in the sense that universities in the United States were in varying stages of development, with each of the then 48 states developing a number of its own universities. These developing universities had serious problems of recruitment, since those with the greatest research talent sought the established universities (Ben-David and Zloczower, 1962). The result was that research talent, for the most part, was very unevenly distributed and concentrated in the more prestigious and highly developed institutions; this condition persists today, although it is undergoing change. An additional factor which influenced the availability of research talent within sociology itself was the ever expanding technological development in the United States in the post World War II period. Such expansion, particularly in industry, drained talent from many academic fields (Gaston, 1973). A major difference between Swedish and American universities in this connection is that the number of faculty necessary for staffing has always been small in Sweden in comparison with America. Thus, the problem of staffing a university with competent, research personnel has been far less in Sweden. Indeed, Sweden, like many other European countries, has had more sociologists capable of research than it could absorb at any one time; while in America for a long period following World War II this was not the case. Thus, while sociological research had a good opportunity to develop at any university in Sweden, the same was not true in America, where many colleges and universities simply had inadequate researchers. Finally, there are particular characteristics of American society which can place special burdens on the development of research and research talent. America is a society which has competing demands, more than most, on the role of the researcher. A large number of middle class, democratic families have demands on the husband's time and attention. The ideal family, among these people, includes a husband–father who maintains family interests, and who is willing to spend time with his family, and contribute time to the church and school. The existence of these competing demands results in family discord, in role conflict for the researcher, and in many instances diminished research activity. As a result there are many influences that run counter to the dedication which may be necessitated by the demands of research in the United States. These general points, concerned with universities in general, have had a major impact on the growth and development of research within academic units, such as sociology departments in the United States. They have constituted serious obstacles to the development of sociological research.

We have dealt with the role of graduate training, graduate student motivation and professional socialization and factors which have placed burdens on the development of research in sociology. Yet in any society, regardless of the conditions, the number of those who can commit themselves to research careers is limited. Basically researchers have not addressed themselves to the problem of what is involved at the social-psychological level to commit oneself to research and scientific work. We are obviously not talking about the individual who produces an article or two, or even a book, for his entire career. What are the ingredients involved? There are at least three broad dimensions. A first is the matter of dedication and commitment, the discipline involved in completing a task. A second is the capacity to tolerate ambiguity and frustration. For example, research involves a gamble, one doesn't know how it will turn out; will anyone want to publish it? How many rejections from a journal can one tolerate before the entire process becomes too painful? The third dimension is more complex, since it involves the previous two dimensions, plus the capacity to liberate creative forces. These are the innovators, they possess the dedication; they possess a tolerance for frustration; but they also have a rare gift of innovation. The nature and process of innovation involves basically the ability to see new relationships out of old configurations. It is also a matter of how one configuration leads to another. It is not only the capacity to visualize a new configuration, but to explore and develop it into a piece of work that clarifies and can be integrated. This is the essential difference between the dilettante and the innovator. Probably the greatest single barrier to innovation is the personality gestalt which is brought to bear. Here we find life styles which are difficult to break. If there is a basic conflict within the human personality, it probably takes the form of a contest between that aspect of personality which has accommodated to life and that innovative component looking for new experience. Whenever the human personality has learned to accommodate, a basic life process, it is inevitably at the expense of having abandoned some other set of wishes. When Blacks accommodated to the pattern of race, they gave up other goals. It may well have been realistic, but this is not the issue. So it is with all people, accommodation is inevitable and necessary. Yet, it also means that the unknown, in terms of creative resources, has to struggle in order to emerge. It is this central problem which is confusing, misunderstood and difficult. This is why creativity invariably produces anxiety. And this is why many are unable to produce scientific work of stature. These aspects of research commitment are not sufficiently dealt with or understood. Unless we are able to do so research careers, at least in sociology, will continue to be limited to very small numbers.

There are other problems within sociology itself which have never been resolved and which continue to have an impact on the development of research and the commitment of sociologists to a research career. As sociologists we have still not decided on what the scope and aim of sociology is. What the range of acceptable methodologies is. Even standards for acceptable work are more variable than in the more established fields (Gaston, 1973). With regard to the scope and aim of sociology, the very fact that it remains a socially sensitive discipline means that the direction of sociology is determined less by the internal gaps in sociological knowledge and more by what society may consider important at the moment. Once such a goal is accepted whatever research orientations are present to change, the emphasis is really on action to ameliorate and research at best is employed to support action. Under these circumstances there is less patience with systematically studying major gaps in sociological knowledge, and there is impatience about studying such areas as carefully as they should be. In addition, the existence among sociologists of a perspective for the reform of social ills means that sociological goals are primarily to direct and produce social changes. Inherent disappointments are created for several reasons. To influence social change in any society is less a function of research knowledge and science, and is much more a matter of economic and political decision making, and these are slow, complicated and likely to create disappointment about the contribution which research can make. Certainly it can be argued that only a small amount of the significant social legislation in America, or any society, is a result of sociological research. If anything, major social issues are decided less by research and much more by political decision making which rests on the power of particular constituencies. Moreover, if one takes a view of history there is considerable evidence to show that major social changes were created by men and events that had little to do with the rational and orderly collection of data. The point is that given such reformistic goals, noble in themselves, one may also find unintended effects which work against the development of research interests in sociology.

The failure to resolve central issues of concern as to the nature of sociology has given rise to some major problems which, if not resolved, may continue to drain the energies of sociologists in directions that work against sociology's development, at least in the long run. One such development is noted in a tendency to become increasingly preoccupied with what may be identified as the "sociology of sociology". Such concerns are significant, and are a necessary ingredient, if sociology is to develop. Yet the writing which has appeared in the last decade devoted to "what is wrong with sociology", including "why sociologists study what they study" is formidable. In time it could absorb a significant amount of sociological concern and may replace the basic research task of dealing with data, hard or soft.

A second trend which reflects an unresolved set of issues is the reappearance of an old issue, the controversy of "hard data" versus "soft data", case study versus quantitative sociology. This controversy presumably settled some several decades ago has arisen once more. The current phrase, humanistic sociology, which is not clearly defined, and which subsumes all these components of soft data, came out of a strong German philosophical tradition in Europe. In America, which has always been lacking philosophy there was no similar philosophical background. America's philosophical contribution to the methodological controversy came from the pragmatism of John Dewey. Pragmatism, which took hold in American academic life, found its expression in the development of empirical sociology with Franklin Giddings at Columbia University, a sociologist who spent considerable time helping social agencies develop ways of studying statistically the social problems of people in the 1920's. Thus, through the late 1920's, 1930's and 1940's the controversy of humanistic sociology versus empirical was experienced at all leading departments of sociology. At different times one position or the other has been in ascendance, although for the most empirical sociology was in ascendance in the 1950's. The reemergence of the so-called humanistic approach in American sociology today represents not only a response to what some believe are mechanistic methods of empiricism, but an ideological response as well, since humanists are interested in examining and dealing with the feelings in data, reacting to what is perceived as impersonal attitudes toward the people being studied. Qualitative analysis, however, has its own special problems. If one hopes to get closer to the feelings of people by such techniques as placing oneself in the "role of the other", one has to have the emotional and intellectual capacity to do so. Can the alienated person, the neurotic person, place himself in another's position without projecting and experiencing things that may not be there at all? There is always a real problem of the distortion of data, and a real possibility that such people may not be in touch with the feelings of people at all. (Are we to screen those who deal with qualitative analysis to see that they are free of neurotic conflicts? Certainly the suggestion is unrealistic.) Why the resurgence of humanistic sociology at the present time? In part such a response has to be seen as a general reaction of students to the establishment, to establishment sociology seen as statistical, to rigidity which quantitative sociology represents for these people. Viewed in these essentially negative terms, it becomes a way of justifying other methods. But one has to suggest that for many sociologists, humanistic sociology is less an expression of regard for people, a better way to understand, and more a concern for avoiding the rigors required of any set of methods, quantitative or qualitative. Further, if on the one hand the rules for gathering data can be rejected because they are non-humanistic, then it is any one's game to play with any set of rules. The suspicion that humanistic sociology, as employed by some, does not represent a concern for understanding people can be noted in the nature of projects, themselves. The considerable preoccupation of sociologists with the reinterpretation of what sociological pioneers, long since dead, "really meant" suggests this. In reality good work can come out of any methodological tradition. Nevertheless, until sociology can resolve some of the issues regarding its scope and aim, its methodology, its standards, sociologists will drain the energies of their members into issues that may be socially relevant but unproductive in regard to the building of a discipline. We cannot tell whether the tendencies we have discussed merely reflect the immaturity of sociology as a science. Perhaps other sciences experienced similar problems at an earlier stage of their development. We shall have to await further research on this question.

From all that has been said we can see that the improvement of the research capacity in sociology is complex. As a result there is a great reserve of faculty in sociology departments who are neither trained for nor committed to research. Moreover, to the extent that what we have is also true for other fields, there are special difficulties for any university that wishes to undergo change. To move from a university with a teaching-service orientation to one which seeks to upgrade research and publication means a drastic shift and calls for competence not readily available. Few university administrators are capable of dealing with the turmoil that may take place. The inertia, the resistance and the antagonisms generated among a faculty are sufficient to demoralize even the most competent administrator. One way faculty have of dealing with a system that promises differential rewards for the relatively few involved in research and publication is the formation of teachers' unions. The effect is to provide job security and economic rewards for that segment of the faculty that would not ordinarily obtain them in a reward system based on research and publication. The danger that a reward system based on longevity and seniority, rather than research and publication, could depress the interest and motivation of a faculty to engage in research is formidable.

A final comment on a factor that will influence the development of research careers in sociology and other fields is related to fiscal constraints and the administrative personnel who have been brought in to deal with these. The expansion of research in the United States, which was pronounced in the 1950's and 1960's is likely to be less in the next decade. Fiscal problems in the economy have influenced the general allotment of funds and new educational administrators, with a managerial orientation, exemplify such views (Snyder, 1973). We cannot predict with any certainty that research will suffer in all institutions, but it is reasonable to expect that it will not continue to hold a high priority. Moreover, while some administrators with a managerial orientation may be sympathetic to research, they cannot be expected to devote major portions of their energy to furthering research, when their task is over-all management of limited funds (Thompson, 1967). In the "crunch" educational funds will go first for teaching. This is true for most private, as well as publicly supported, institutions. It is easy to justify and easy to manage. Why and how such persons have moved into positions of authority in the university setting is in itself interesting. First, the size of many public universities requires organizational skills that transcend the interests and skills of those involved in a scholarly career. Thus, the very size of the university budget has resulted in a public demand for an accounting of the money. Public concern was aggravated by student rioting in recent years, and the belief arose that the university in general requires greater public surveillance. Fiscal constraints will at least for the short run have the impact of curtailing research in sociology, and fiscal constraints will discourage those who may seek a career in research. On the other hand, one can look on this period of relative austerity as one in which researchers can reexamine themselves and what they are about. They may discover that many projects were ill conceived, had inflated budgets and, in many instances, produced barren findings (Orlans, 1962). If such self examination were to occur, it might serve to produce better research and better researchers. It might also serve to increase the researchers' responsibility to the university and the public at large (Nisbet, 1971: 171–196).

Bibliography

Ben-David, Joseph and Zloczower, Awraham, 1962. Universities and academic systems in modern societies. *European Journal of Sociology*, III, 45–84.

Blau, Peter M. and Scott, W. Richard, 1962. *Formal Organizations*. San Francisco: Chandler Publishing Co.

Caplow, Theodore, 1964. *Principles of Organization*. New York: Harcourt, Brace, and World.

Etzioni, Amitai, 1961. *A Comparative Analysis of Complex Organizations*. New York: Free Press of Glencoe.

Gaston, Jerry, 1973. The Problems of Achieving Excellence in a University Context. Unpublished manuscript.

Gross, Edward and Grambsch, Paul V., 1968. *University Goals and Academic Power*. Washington, D.C.: American Council on Education.

Nisbet, Robert, 1971. *The Degradation of the Academic Dogma: The University in America, 1945–1970*. New York: Basic Books, Inc.

Orlans, Harold, 1962. *Effects of Federal Programs on Higher Education*. Washington: The Brookins Institution.

Snyder, Charles R., 1973. Social Characteristics of the New University Administrator. Unpublished manuscript.

Thompson, James D., 1967. *Organizations in Action*. New York: McGraw-Hill Book Co.

Chapter 2

The academic community as a communication system

Torgny T Segerstedt

My thesis is that the scientific or academic community is a communication system. Its main business is to communicate about data, theories and scientific behavior. Scientific knowledge is a matter of cooperation; there is no place for an individual experience, however intense it may be, if it cannot be communicated and repeated. Communication and repetition is what characterizes scientific behavior. Repetitive behavior may be different in different fields of knowledge. In experimental science it must be possible to repeat the experiment, in historical research it must be possible to re-interpret the source-material.

The question then is: what does my thesis that the academic community is a communication system imply? Which are the general presuppositions of a communication system? It seems evident that words as symbols play a central role in communication and our next question for that reason is: how do words acquire meaning, that is, what is the meaning of meaning? In my book *The Nature of Social Reality* (Stockholm 1966) I have tried to answer that question more fully. In this paper I can only give a summary of my view, which evidently is an eclectic one.

My first concern is the relation between words and objects. In the socialization process the child is introduced into the *symbolic environment* of the group into which it has been born. That does mean that he is taught to react towards a phenomenon in a specific way. The total reaction does contain behavior, emotional reaction and verbal behavior. It is important to understand that these different aspects of behavior form a firmly integrated whole. The reaction toward the physical phenomenon *snake* does include flight-behavior, fear and the *word* snake. The physical object snake is regarded as having the quality of being poisonous, dangerous and as having the name of *snake*. The word as such is regarded as a quality or property of the object. The unique thing with the verbal behavior is that at the same time as it is integrated with the total responses towards the stimulus, it is abstracted from the total situation and is regarded as a symbol of that situation.

The unique nature of language has not been made explicit by the statement that it is a part of the mass of social behavior. The essential step is taken when a behavior-pattern or attitude is established towards the word *as a word*. To some extent that stage is commenced when you try to acquire correct verbal behavior; but in all kinds of behavior you are trained to behave correctly. Verbal behavior is unique in so far as you learn to employ the word as something distinct from the object. You are not taught to do that with qualities such as blue, soft or square. There are social customs established towards words. Words are part of a total reaction and at the same time abstracted from that situation, which enables a word to be *a symbol of the total mass of reactions*. The implication of this concept of symbol is that by a symbol you can stimulate not only other human beings but you can stimulate yourself as well. At the same time I believe it to be important to point out that the power of a symbol is limited to the group in which the human being is socialized. The *word cow* may be associated with beefsteak, milk and rural life in our culture, but in other cultures it is associated with holiness and worship.

This last statement leads us to another important psychological observation with regard to the formation of symbols. We may say that the total reaction towards an object means structuring the idea of reality of the subject. We know that reality is experienced in different ways in different cultures and human groups. But one must note that the socialization process means structuring of the self as well. The socialization process does imply that social customs are formed, the new member of the group is taught how to behave in an actual situation as well as in expected ones. We teach not only observable behavior, but dispositions are formed as well. If we say that customs have two elements: behavior which is observable and dispositions, which are assumed, when we have made suppositions about the self or the personality, we presuppose that dispositions are mutually integrated and consequently shape or structure ego.

In order to understand a communication-system I believe it to be important to distinguish between *meaning* and *function*. The function of words used in communication and social interaction is to create dispositions of customs or to release social behavior. In this sense the function of words is an operative force. But communication is often indirect, that is, the symbol is transmitted from one person to another, who in his turn again transfers it to a third person. This is possible because words have a meaning separate from their function. Sometimes, for example, the function is to arouse emotions rather than to elicit behavior. This is possible because words are associated not only with behavior but with emotions as well. Meaning may be said to be a dispositional quality.

When a word has the same meaning for two or more individuals they belong to the same symbolic environment. That does mean the individuals have internalized the rules of verbal behavior in the same way as other social customs. Social customs imply an integrated or internalized set of social norms. A common symbolic environment is founded on a common system of social norms or rules. For that reason, if you belong to a common symbolic environment you can be said to belong to a common social group, as my definition of group is the following: By group we mean two or more persons with common customs and in interaction because they obey the same social norms, that is, norms which can be traced back to one and the same norm-source (norm-speaker).

There evidently are three main elements in my group-concept: (1) The uniform behavior (social customs), (2) the social norms, that is language-expressions with an imperative function, and (3) the norm-source or the norm-speaker. The norm-source has got a double function: (a) to express and interpret the norms and (b) to enforce them by other promising rewards or by threatening with sanctions. The declaration that individuals A and B belong to the same symbolic environment implies that A and B understand reality by their mutual communication-relation (Cr). At the same time I think it correct to say that Cr has reality only by A and B. This view has been developed by Walter Buckley in a very stimulating manner in his book *Sociology and Modern System Theory* (New Jersey 1967, p. 44 f.).

We started this essay by saying that words are central elements in a communication system. We have found that if words as symbols have the same meaning for two or more persons, that does mean that the persons in question belong to the same system of rules, that is, to the same social group. The communication system is a kind of social group. For that reason it is meaningful to ask the following question: Are there other qualities of a group which are of importance for our main theme, that is, the academic community as a communication system? I have suggested that we in all social groups can discern three basic qualities or functions of a group. These basic functions are the following: (1) the reproductive function, (2) the socialization function, and (3) the productive function. These functions must be realized in all social groups if the group is going to survive. That is a general sociological statement and it is valid for a nation as well as for an association of stamp-collectors.

In a society there may be different groups fulfilling different functions, as for example the family group around the reproductive function, schools and universities fulfilling the socializing function, and working groups in factories or offices carrying out the productive function. In some societies the functions are carried out in the same group; that is the case in an agricultural society which may be called a one-group society. In an industrial society there are three separate groups and the society can be called a three-group society.

What is the bearing of these arguments with regard to the academic or scientific community? We have already found that as a communication system it must be classified as a social group. That is, there must be specific social customs in the scientific community, it must have a common norm system and there must be a common norm-source of some kind. Furthermore the scientific community must fulfill the three basic group functions.

I think the best way of approaching the problem is to start with the three basic functions. Reproduction is with regard to the academic community a matter of recruiting students. That function has most evidently been an enormous problem for all universities during the 'sixties. They have experienced the increasing number of new students coming up to the universities, which have developed from universities to multiversities. It is well known what this has meant with regard to overcrowding, teacher shortage and anonymity of students, all factors which have caused the student unrest. (Note my paper The Situation of Swedish Universities in *The Task of Universities in a Changing World*, Notre Dame, 1971.) But it has also meant problems with regard to internalization of the rules of the academic community—that is, it has caused difficulties with regard to socialization. Socialization means in this case the learning of the meaning of scientific concepts, that is, the meaning of words used in research, the formulation of theory and the verification of hypothesis. This may be said to be a very theoretical procedure. If you look upon the meaning of words you can say that they may be located on a continuum with purely emotional words at one pole and purely theoretical words at the other. The main function of religious words (as used in hymns, for example) is to arouse feelings, the main function of scientific words (as in physics, for example) is to stimulate theoretical behavior. That is true, but perhaps not the whole truth. When integrating scientific or theoretical behavior it is evidently important to internalize a value standard at the same time. A member of an academic community must learn to regard as fundamental the rules and codes as to how to seek the truth and nothing but the truth, that is, never to falsify his reports or to suppress his findings even if they are contrary to his beliefs or dangerous with regard to the activities of political, religious or financial pressure-groups or even harmful for his own reputation as scientist. The socialization process in the academic community is the same as in every other social group, in so far as the new member is under pressure from a norm system which structures his overt behavior as well as his emotional and verbal behavior. But I believe that there are peculiar chracteristics with regard to the norm-system of the academic community, which ought to be mentioned. The first thing that ought to be pointed out is the fact that the academic community as a communication system is international. That is typical for scientific groups in contradistinction from groups with religious or magical function. Robert K. Merton has pointed out that science is characterized by "four sets of institutional imperatives: universalism, communism, disinterestedness, organized scepticism" (*Social Theory and Social Structure*, 1968, page 605). The object of scientific work is to create an international concept-system, an international language and an international culture of its own. That is the reason why there sometimes may be tensions between the scientific community and the political, religious, or economic establishments. The language of physics is (or ought to be) the same in Uppsala, Berkeley, Peking and Nairobi. And the same is true with regard to the language of economics. That does mean that our efforts to socialize new members imply that we teach them the international meaning of words used in science. That is a *conditio qua non* of all learned communication. Historically we can point out that different kinds of power elites have tried to isolate a country from the international community. But that has never been successful or at least successful only for a short while. This international education is going on in national universities and it gives universities all over the world a particular status in a nation: a university is the institution of higher education inside the nation and it has the responsibility of performing the higher education of the nation. Yet at the same time it is a member of an international system and it is only by being such a participant that the university has value for the nation. Its

23

membership in the international system is a condition of its carrying out its national function. The university is acting as an observer and rapporteur of what is going on in the international field of research and learning. On the other hand, the international system of scientific rules is the subject of examination and adjustment. The norm-system of the academic or scientific community is always an *open one*. Every competent person may enter it and revise it, the academic community is an open group. This fact influences the structure of the norm-source. I think that we can say that because of the openness of the norm-system, every member of the academic community is a norm-source and responsible for the validity of the scientific behavior of the group. That is the reason why the integration of the norm-system into the group member is so important in higher education. That may also explain why it is so important to internalize the value-standard. Every member of the academic community must be trained to take over the responsibility of the norm-system and the moral standard of research. Consequently no scientists can approve of any non-scientific government of research.

The third basic function is that of *production*. That function is with regard to the scientific group, the production and communication of new facts and truths. The activity must be carried out according to the general rules of the academic community, that is, the autonomy of scientific research must be respected. By autonomy I mean the right of scholars to decide and choose (1) the objects of research, (2) the methods, theories and concepts to be used in research, and (3) to evaluate the fundamental scientific value of the results obtained. The value of the results with regard to application in society may be valued by others. I believe that points (2) and (3) are the most important with regard to the independence of science and they do not permit any kind of compromising. With reference to point (1) I think it is possible to accept that non-scientific institutions may ask for certain kinds of research to be carried out as long as they do not tamper with (2) and (3). But of course there must always be means and possibilities for basic research, that is, members of the scientific community must have a chance of choosing the object of research as well. An important principle to which insufficient attention has been paid is the following, which ought to be carefully observed by social scientists: the level of the theoretical system of Science, in terms of inclusiveness, coherence, etc., determines the degree of autonomy of science. Few politicians of today would try to influence a scientist working in the field of physics or chemistry as these sciences have developed strong theoretical systems. But as long as only miniature theories or theories of middle range are available in social sciences, a considerable risk of exertion of outside pressure remains. Therefore I find it dangerous that social scientists have so little concern for theoretical and epistemological problems. I draw the following practical conclusions: the stronger the theoretical framework of a discipline the less will the "autonomy risk" be for scientists participating in applied research. I think it could also be stated that a coherent theoretical system is an unconditional demand for an accumulation of knowledge, that is for communication of results of research and research methods.

I have pointed out the difference between the strong theoretical system of sciences such as physics and chemistry and the theoretical systems of sociology and economy. These facts draw the attention to a characteristic trait of academic communication: it has many sub-groups or sub-cultures. There must for that reason most evidently be a risk that there will appear communication difficulties between the different sub-groups. Or perhaps it is more honest to say that in many cases there does not exist any communication at all between different departments or fields of research. There is a common agreement about the value of autonomy of research and of the importance of a coherent and well-defined set of concepts, but no real communication.

We all accept certain emotionally loaded norms which create we-feeling and which stress the general importance of our work. The academic community has many rites and ceremonies. There are general rules regarding how the socialization process ought to be carried out and the best way of teaching and creating motivation. But every science seems to have specific rules of its own. The consequence is that it is easier for a physicist in Uppsala to communicate with his colleagues in Berkeley, Moscow, Peking or Cairo than with his colleagues in the sociology department just across the street. An historian or a social scientist may be as ignorant about what is going on in the laboratories in the physics department as the man in the street. These different or specific systems of rules which are valid in academic fields of research make it difficult to organize interdisciplinary research within universities. One should however distinguish between genuine and pseudo-interdisciplinary research. *Genuine interdisciplinary* research presupposes a common theoretical basis, shared by two or more disciplines, which is a relatively rare case. It ought however to be more closely studied if new fields of research do not emerge when two or more scientists from different areas of research try to find a common language or common set of rules for the borderlines between their subjects. If such a new specific system of rules is established we cannot speak about interdisciplinary research. We have in reality a new academic discipline in its own right.

With the term *pseudo-interdisciplinary* I refer to research in which specialists from different disciplines collaborate, each applying his own methods and theories, in order to study a problem. The latter type of research is common in, e.g., applied medical research and can easily be organized in social science. I think we should decide what kind of inter-disciplinary research we want to realize. Interdisciplinary research with a common theoretical frame of reference has been the vision, but in reality only interdisciplinary cooperation has taken place.

I started this essay by saying that scientific knowledge is a matter of cooperation and communication. That does mean that research and education, by its very definition, is concerned with knowledge which can be communicated. It does furthermore imply that there must be communication between scholarly education and research, that is, between the two main responsibilities of the academic community. In his interesting book *The Organization of Academic Work* (New York, 1973) Peter M. Blau has pointed out and demonstrated that there is a higher performance rate of academic institutions in which the communication between scholarly research and higher education is well organized. I think it is necessary that the academic community, in order to define its own situation and defend its own structure, study its own characteristics as a sociological phenomenon.

Chapter 3

Comments on the research pattern

Gunnar Boalt, Robert Erikson
and Herman Lantz

Lee Freese (1972, pp. 472–487) and Willer and Willer (1972, pp. 483–486), have each addressed themselves to the problems of developing cumulative knowledge in sociology.

Freese points out at least two causes for the scarcity of cumulative research in sociology. Sociologists differ in theories, paradigms, methods, language, etc. They have not been able to take over the cumulative tradition of the natural sciences, although they often believe that they have. Perhaps this lack of similarity between sociology and the natural sciences might depend on the fact that different paradigms in the natural sciences have resulted in the establishing of different natural sciences, each one with its own paradigm.

A second cause for lack of cumulative, empirical research in sociology is the change in society. Sociological writing may influence the subjects and therefore change the behaviors studied.

On a less ambitious, empirical level we might combine the two causes to a third. Society and social sciences interact. Changes in society mean changes in ideology, and ideology of science. Sociological theories based on a previous ideology are seldom disproved—there is neither time nor interest for that. Instead, they become outmoded, forgotten and replaced by more fashionable ones, oriented toward new problems, approaches and facts dressed in a new terminology adapted to this ideology. Not that it is easy to go back to previous research. The data of previous research are presented according to problems and hypotheses that may be alien to the modern researcher, who finds it exceedingly difficult and time consuming to dig out the relevant results. But most researchers are willing to try—for a while. Their own research is stabilized and legitimized when they are able to present a predecessor, with some of the dust brushed off. Classic writers, still able to command respect, run a greater risk to be incorporated as predecessors. Sociologists tend none the less to be hasty in handling previous literature. They do not at all dislike to claim "innovation", and they hardly take the reproach with skipping earlier work very seriously. Even to return to an old classic writer, suitable for modern ideology and modern problems, is a rediscovery, a kind of innovation. When writers as Karl Marx, Emile Durkheim and Max Weber, translated and slightly adapted to modern terminology, were brought back on the sociological scene, this was considered an important event. And it *was* important, even to us here, as it demonstrates how little sociology has advanced since their days, how far sociology is removed from the cumulative ideal. Sociological writing may, thus, be nearly immortal, if it still is left on some book-shelves and a handy system-builder finds it useful for his purposes. But the overwhelming part of sociological writing is soon forgotten or ignored, which makes it easier and less risky for the new sociologists to claim innovation in spite of the spectacular but few resurrections in the sociological church yards. The point is that the sociologists' drive for innovation not only is a result of the non-cumulative character of sociological research, it also is an obstacle for a change toward the cumulative direction.

Sociological research may influence society and certainly has an ideological function too, for example to defend or to attack the present society, but probably the effects are much stronger in the opposite direction; that is, sociology is so dependent on society and ideology that for example sociology in the Eastern European countries according to Lantz, 1971, differs from that in Western countries. There are probably differences between Western European countries and the United States, and in the same way Western European countries may differ from one another, universities in the same country perhaps too. If so, this would be another obstacle for cumulative research.

Let us stop with these intertwined causes for the lack of cumulative research in sociology. We are far more interested in some of the effects than in the causes.

Sociologists are not only able to present their results as innovations, they are rewarded if they do. Otherwise they might find it difficult to get it appreciated and/or published. For the same reasons they present tables, figures, charts, statistics and so forth in the same manner as do researchers in the natural sciences. This may, in some cases be a simple device to have something published.

A little more permanent success is possible in at least two different ways. One can either build a system, write books about it and suddenly find it popular, or one may rely on articles or books in a promising new field or criticize authorities outside the new area.

System builders must publish good monographs in expanding fields but these must command the attention of many scattered sociologists or they must dominate a large and influential department along with its reading lists. If this happens, the system-builder attains the rank of a successful empire-builder, surrounded by his faithful attendants.

Many try to build an empire out of their position. Few succeed very well. Thus, empire building is a risky business and researchers who do not succeed tend to blame their "jealous" colleagues, their "incompetent" co-workers—sometimes even their own charming persons—for their lack of success. They often tend to attack the scientific establishment that did not reward them.

Those who rely on articles (or books) in new fields either have a good nose for attractive smells or strong teeth for biting criticism. But in both cases they have to abandon their teachers and the systems they were brought up in, until they have reached a position where they might start to construct a system of their own.

We believe that cumulative research is rare in sociology. Sociologists are, as Alvin Gouldner (see *The Coming Crisis in Western Sociology*) and others have stressed, influenced by their society, its ideologies and its problems, but as most of them believe in the myth of the cumulative science they still are eager to influence researchers outside their own sphere and thus adapt their theories, language, terminology and methodology to the best selling usage, thinking more of professional sociologists than of society. In this way some system-builders and empire-builders might, temporarily, cover large, international, areas, although most of them have to be satisfied with a country, a university or a research team, where they might enjoy a short period of success. But the point is that each school or department or team work have to adapt their creed to ideology and problems, to refine their terminology, theories and methods and to publish as many facts in favor of their views as possible, in order to impress friendly readers and make them believe that this research is cumulative.

The following is an attempt to systematize this discussion of the behavior of sociologists:

The lack of accumulation tradition results in:
1. No replications.
2. Few series of theory, method or results refinement.
3. Previous work being ignored and not respected.
4. The production patterns of
   a. Monographs if the authors are able to get them on reading lists, etc. (compare Kuhn, et al.).
   b. Articles, if the authors cannot.
   c. "Interesting innovations", either in expanding fields or critiques.

The formal acceptance of the "natural science" publication technique results in:
5. The same desperate scramble for the best journals, etc.
6. A similar way of stressing what is new (sociologists tend to overdo this).
7. The same amount of citations.
8. A similar use of tables, figures, diagrams, etc.
9. The same wish to be cited, respected, etc.

This means in practice that:
10. Successive accumulation is possible either (a) within an empire that is rewarded with academic degrees, publications, or promotions; (b) in a field using the publication patterns of medicine or the natural sciences.
11. A new field is evacuated when the easy chance of "innovation" is gone.
12. In the long run, few new basic facts emerge out of the research (the circle is a better model than the spiral).
13. Established and aspiring sociologists differ in several ways in that
    a. Established sociologists accept their own research and its setting (it's honest and important). Others tend not to accept this.
    b. Aspiring sociologists question axioms, postulates, theories, results, goals and sometimes scientific method at large.
    c. Established sociologists tend to settle down to a new set of rules, etc., even though they
    d. accept those parts they have use for (i.e., power, system, hierarchy, financial resources, journals, foundations).
    e. How much they may or are willing to take over depends on the strength of the ideological conflict.

Some of the following points could be tested in Sweden with conventional research:

A. Comparisons between productivity patterns in sociology vs. those of the natural sciences.
   1. Sociology professors—many monographs, few articles in good journals.
   2. Natural scientists—accumulate articles that also appear in medical sociology.

B. Academic Career Patterns.
   1. Loyal pupil until acquirement of Ph.D.
   2. Ph.D:s have more independence, critisize harmless outsiders.
   3. Promotion to professor starts system "empire" building.
   4. Different ways out.

C. If Sociology does not advance but only adapts to society and ideology, adherents of different ideologies cannot be expected to evaluate their different research styles and results in the same way.
   1. Established and emergent sociologists differ in postulates, theories, methods, and goals.
   2. These differences are smaller in technical, stable areas and greater in instable areas.

This discussion can be phrased in other terms. Hagstrom (Warren O. Hagstrom: *The Scientific Community,* 1965, p. 11) and Segerstedt (the previous chapter, but also *The Nature of Social Reality* and *Den akademiska gemenskapen*, both printed in Stockholm 1966) discuss the problem in terms such as norms, common to all sciences, particular to each research area and inclusive norms of the given society. Hagstrom relates the space–time independence to the norm-system as follows: "Deviation from vague norms is more likely than deviation from norms specified for a concrete set of practices. It follows that physical scientists are less likely to deviate from the norms of science and scholarship than are social scientists or humanists" (Hagstrom, p. 11). Hendrix gives an example in his study of communication of erroneous material: *Nuclear Family Universality*. We could easily accept Segerstedt's and Hagstrom's approach and their categories, well adapted to explain similarities in scientific norms and differences between societies. We do not, however, since we intend to concentrate our interests on differences in research or publishing behaviors between aggregates forming continuums in time and in space: continents, nations, areas, universities, faculties, departments and research groups. If there are such differences they can, of course, be related to differences in norms, but we confine ourselves to a number of empirical sociological studies, carried out within the frame of reference presented above and formally belonging to the research made possible by grants from The Bank of Sweden Tercentenary Fund (Riksbankens Jubileumsfond) and from the Social Science Research Council in Sweden. The Studies have been made by several co-workers at different levels of aspiration, some of them very restricted in scope and material, some of them more ambitious. They all have in common demonstrable differences in sociological research between areas, time periods, universities and generations using content analysis or small surveys, thus trying to locate some of the barriers against scientific communication and efficient research in sociology. We have taken for granted that large time intervals do create such barriers and so we concentrate instead on similar countries, short time periods, universities near one another and on generations directly following one another, where differences easily are overlooked although they may be considerable and probably disturbing—and far from our research ideal.

Some of these differences are associated with the new paradigms pushed by the student revolt. We are, however, less interested in the paradigms than in their effect on communication on the micro level, removing old barriers and creating new ones.

References

Boalt, Gunnar, 1969. *The Sociology of Research*. Carbondale, Ill.: Southern Illinois University Press.

Boalt, Gunnar and Lantz, Herman, 1970. *Universities and Research*. New York: Wiley.

Boalt, Gunnar, Herlin, Helena and Lantz, Herman, 1973. *The Academic Pattern*, Stockholm: Almqvist & Wiksell.

Freese, Lee, 1972. Cumulative sociological knowledge. *American Sociological Review* 37 (August): 472–482.

Freese, Lee, 1972. Cumulative sociological knowledge, an addendum. *American Sociological Review* 37 (August): 486–487.

Gouldner, Alvin, 1971. *The Coming Crisis of Western Sociology*. New York.

Hagstrom, Warren O., 1965. *The Scientific Community*. Basic Books.

Kuhn, Thomas S., 1962. *The Structure of Scientific Revolutions*. Chicago: The University of Chicago Press.

Lantz, Herman, 1972. *The State of Sociology in Eastern Europe.* Carbondale, Ill.: Southern Illinois University Press.

Segerstedt, Torgny, 1966. Den akademiska gemenskapen. (The Academic Community). Uppsala: Almqvist & Wiksell.

Segerstedt, Torgny, 1966. *The Nature of Social Reality.* Totowa, N. J.: The Bedminster Press.

Willer, David and Judith, 1972. Why sociological knowledge is not cumulative;— a reply to Freese *American Sociological Review* 37 (August): 483–486.

Chapter 4

Regional differences in articles on the sociology of art

Gunnar Boalt and Paul Lindblom

In other sections of this book we have tried to deal with different facets of research. In the present chapter which deals with the sociology of art, including literature and music, we report on an analysis of 41 articles. These research areas are not very popular in the United States. Only 10 out of our 41 articles are published in American Journals, one in a Canadian, 14 in British or French Journals and 16 in *Kölner Zeitschrift für Soziologie und Sozialpsychologie* (West Germany). This makes it possible to compare research patterns (as expressed in the articles) in the United States (and Canada) with Western Europe and then, in the same way to compare West Germany with England and France.

Our sample was taken out of 66 journals, devoted to sociology or at least giving access to it. We excluded articles on art, irrelevant for the modern, Western societies. Historical and anthropological articles are included only if they have a direct bearing on our own conditions. The special journals for museums and libraries have also been passed by.

In order to concentrate on recent material we have limited our sample to volumes published in 1969–1972. *Kölner Zeitschrift für Soziologie* gave us 16 articles, *Archives Européennes de Sociologie* 7, *British Journal of Sociology* 4, *Public Opinion Quarterly* (Princeton, N.J., USA), *American Scholar* (Washington, D.C., USA), *American Sociological Review* (New York, USA), *Editorial Research Reports* (USA), *Journal of American Folklore* (Richmond, Virginia, USA), *Journal of Human Relations* (Wilberforce, Ohio, USA), *Journal of Social Issues* (New York, USA) and *Sociological Inquiry* (Toronto, Canada) one each.

This material will be used to test a hypothesis built on the discussion in

Table 1. *Data on 6 variables from our three samples (USA–Canada, England–France and West Germany)*

Articles printed in			Sum
	Statistics or tables	No statistics or tables	
USA and Canada	5	6	11
England, France and West Germany	7	23	30
England and France	5	9	14
West Germany	2	14	16
Sum	12	29	41
	"Innovation"	No innovation	
USA and Canada	6	5	11
England, France and West Germany	6	24	30
England and France	3	11	14
West Germany	3	13	16
Sum	12	29	41
	Exemplification	No exemplification	
USA and Canada	4	7	11
England, France and West Germany	23	7	30
England and France	10	4	14
West Germany	13	3	16
Sum	27	14	41
	Over-all studies	Not over-all studies	
USA and Canada	3	8	11
England, France and West Germany	17	13	30
England and France	5	9	14
West Germany	12	4	16
Sum	20	21	41

the previous chapter: sociological research in the Western countries tends to show differences in paradigms and/or publication techniques between regions and even between neighbour-countries.

Our general knowledge of the sociological journals made us suspect that American and Canadian articles—owing to the harder competition

Number of references

Articles printed in	0	1	2	3	4	5	6	7	8	9	10	11	12	13	14	15	16	17	18	19	20	21	22	23	24	25	26–30	35–35	36–40	41–45	46–50	51–60	61–70	71–80	80
USA and Canada		1				1																								1					1
England, France and West Germany	3						1		2	1				2		1	1	1	1	1	1				2		3	1	1		1	4	2		
England and France	1								1					2				1	1	1	1				1		2	1	1		1	3	2	2	2
West Germany	2								1	1				2		1			1	1	1				1		1	1			1	1	2	2	3
Sum	4	1				2	1		2	1		1	1	3	1	2	1	2	2	1	1				2		3	1	1	1	4	4	2	2	3

Number of pages

Articles printed in	4	5	6	7	8	9	10	11	12	13	14	15	16	17	18	19	20	21	22	23	24	25	26	27	28	29	30	31	32	33	34	35	35
USA and Canada				1		1	1	2	2	2	2	2		2															2				
England, France and West Germany	1	1	1		5	1			2	3	2	3		1	1	1	1	2	2	1									1				
England and France	1	1	1		2		1			2	2			1	1	1	1	1	1	1									1				
West Germany	1	1	1		3		1		3			1		1	1		1		1										2				
Sum	1	1	2		6	1	4	2	3	4	3	3		1	1	1	2	2	2	1									2				

for acceptance and space—should be comparatively short resulting in fewer references and often use of statistics or tables thus being able to claim (directly or indirectly) "innovation". Less often exemplification is used to demonstrate their point or the article assumes the character of an over-all study.

We proceed to classify our notes on the articles in order to measure six variables: (1) use of statistics or tables, (2) presenting data as "innovations" or not, (3) using exemplification to support the representation, or not, (4) giving an over-all review of the field, (5) number of references, (6) number of pages. How do our samples from USA (and Canada), Western Europe (England, France) and West Germany come out in these respects? We present our data in table 1.

This table indicates that our American sample, more often than our European sample tends to use statistics or tables (5/11 versus 7/30) and more often, generally with the aid of the tables, can be said to claim innovation (6/11 versus 6/30), but less often to use exemplification (4/11 versus 23/30) or over-all studies (3/11 versus 17/30), to occupy fewer pages (the arithmetic mean is 13 pages versus 16) and—probably as a consequence—give a smaller number of references (the mean is 22 versus 32). This support allows us to proceed to the corresponding differences between England and France on the one hand, West Germany on the other.

We expect that England and France, more related than West Germany to the United States should differ in research pattern from West Germany in the same directions as the United States differs from the three European countries. The table shows that England and France together tend toward a research or publication pattern parallel to that of the United States as far as statistics (5/14 versus 2/16), "innovation" (3/14 versus 3/16), exemplification (10/14 versus 13/16) and over-all studies (5/14 versus 12/16) are concerned, but this does not hold for number of references (arithmetic means 39 versus 26) or number of pages (means 19 versus 14).

This discussion has a flaw. On the one hand we assume that the United States research/publication pattern should differ from that of England, France and West Germany, on the other hand England and France, should replicate the American pattern in relation to West Germany. But suppose that our sample from England and France in some respects should be more American than our sample from USA and Canada? Evidently we have to formulate our expectations more explicitly and compare our three samples (from America, England–France and West

Table 2. *Percentages and means for six variables in three samples of articles*

Sample from	Statistics (1)	Innovation (2)	Exemplification (3)	Over-all studies (4)	References (5)	Pages (6)
USA–Canada	45%	55%	36%	27%	22	13
England–France	36%	21%	71%	36%	39	19
West Germany	13%	19%	81%	75%	26	14

Germany) in all six respects. The sample from USA and Canada should have the highest rates for statistics and innovation, the lowest for exemplification and over-all studies, the lowest means of number of pages and of references. The sample from West Germany should be at the opposite end, and the Anglo-French sample take an intermediate position all the way through. We construct table 2 to test this hypothesis.

This allows us 12 comparisons of research patterns, 6 between the American sample and the Anglo-French, 6 between the Anglo-French pattern and the West German. The first 6 all come out as they should, but 2 out of the later 6 do not: in respect to number of references and pages the Anglo-French sample does not lie between the American and the West German means. Ten cases out of twelve, thus, support our hypotheses. From a statistical point that is not so bad. If we could consider these 12 comparisons independent of one another the probability that this could happen by chance is less than 1 in 50. But actually statistics and innovation are probably coupled with one another, which should raise the probability. References and pages also should be highly correlated and we could then reduce the two diverging cases a step, thus keeping the probability on a low level. Our hypothesis that Western countries do differ in research patterns, and differ less the nearer they are, can not be refuted by these data.

What do we mean then by research and/or publication patterns? We believe that in the United States and Canada a research report tends to be higher valued if statistics are used for testing hypotheses or supporting ideas, in the same way as we have used them here in order to make our pilot study more respectable. In the same way we hope to have made an "innovation" and so given the study more value. We have not tried to use exemplification to support our ideas, neither do we want to support them with a long review of previous efforts in this particular field, with many literature references or many pages. In our opinion the tables and the tactfully hidden claim on innovation are important values, but exemplification, over-all studies, many references and many pages are less important to us. And so we seem to follow the American research or publication pattern we have described above.

Evidently the European sample does not assign the same high regard to statistics and innovation as the American one, but instead more regard to exemplification, over-all studies, many references and pages. We interpret this to mean that they tend to allocate their research resources another way, giving more time and effort to penetration and discussion of their problem and less to data collection and treatment. If so, statistics and the claim of innovation should tend to follow one another (which is more than likely) and in the same way the other four dimensions should be associated (also very likely). When we use the term research pattern for such tendencies we do not only expect that research values should flock together in a number of groups, the values in each group positively associated or correlated with one another, we also expect values from different groups or clusters to be negatively correlated as these groups or clusters of values compete with one another for the researchers' time, and resources. The more researchers allocate to one cluster of research values, the less is left to other clusters.

This idea is built on the "summation" theory, used also in most of the other contributions to this book. Here we have to add that it can be used in this simple form only if the studied sample is rather homogeneous. In this case the sample can be considered homogeneous as it is drawn from articles on the sociology of art, published in Western journals during the years 1968–1972. We can then test the summation theory with our material, if we compute the correlations between our six variables: geographical area, innovation claim, exemplification, over-all studies, number of references and number of pages. We intend to use Yule's Q-coefficients to compute the correlations, and then have to divide each of our variables dichotomically. Areas, use and non-use of statistics, claim on innovation or not, exemplification or not, over-all studies or not, are already divided so, but numbers of references and numbers of pages both have to be split on lower numbers and higher numbers. Looking at their distributions in table 1, we find a gap in the reference table near the median, as no articles have given 21, 22 or 23 references and we then consider less than 21 references as few, more than 23 as many. The distribution of pages is more concentrated near the median, but there are only two articles with 13 pages and so we say that 13 and less pages are

Table 3. *Matrix of correlations in a sample of 41 Western sociological articles, 1968–72*

	Statistics	Innovation	Exempli-fication	Over-all articles	Number of references	Number of pages
	Yes No	Yes No	Yes No	Yes No	>13 <21	>13 <14
United States and Canada / England, France, West Germany	5|6 / 7|23 +.50	6|5 / 6|24 +.66	4|7 / 23|7 −.70	3|8 / 17|13 −.55	2|9 / 16|14 −.67	4|7 / 18|12 −.44
Statistics (or tables) Yes / No		11|1 / 1|28 +1	6|6 / 21|8 −.43	1|11 / 19|10 −.91	5|7 / 13|16 −.11	6|6 / 16|13 −.10
Innovation claim Yes / No			5|7 / 23|7 −.63	1|11 / 19|10 −.91	5|7 / 13|10 −.11	6|6 / 16|13 −.10
Exemplification Yes / No				16|11 / 4|10 +.57	14|13 / 4|10 +.46	16|11 / 6|11 +.32
Over-all articles Yes / No					9|11 / 9|12 +.04	12|8 / 10|11 +.25
Number of references >23 <21 >13						15|3 / 7|16 +.84
Number of pages <14						

Table 4. *Matrix of correlations in a sample of 30 European sociological articles, 1968–72*

	Statistics	Innovation	Number of references	Number of pages	Exemplification	Over-all articles
	Yes No	Yes No	>23 <21	>13 <14	Yes No	Yes No
England and France West Germany	$\frac{5\,|\,9}{2\,|\,14}$ +.59	$\frac{3\,|\,11}{1\,|\,13}$ +.08	$\frac{10\,|\,4}{6\,|\,10}$ +.60	$\frac{11\,|\,3}{7\,|\,9}$ +.65	$\frac{10\,|\,4}{13\,|\,3}$ −.27	$\frac{5\,|\,9}{12\,|\,4}$ −.69
Statistics (or tables) Yes No		$\frac{6\,|\,1}{0\,|\,23}$ +1	$\frac{5\,|\,2}{11\,|\,12}$ +.46	$\frac{6\,|\,1}{12\,|\,11}$ +.69	$\frac{4\,|\,3}{19\,|\,4}$ −.56	$\frac{1\,|\,6}{16\,|\,7}$ −.86
Innovation claim Yes No			$\frac{4\,|\,2}{12\,|\,12}$ +.33	$\frac{4\,|\,2}{14\,|\,10}$ +.18	$\frac{3\,|\,3}{20\,|\,4}$ −.69	$\frac{0\,|\,6}{17\,|\,7}$ −1
Number of references 23 21				$\frac{13\,|\,3}{5\,|\,9}$ +.77	$\frac{12\,|\,4}{11\,|\,3}$ −.10	$\frac{8\,|\,8}{9\,|\,5}$ −.29
Number of pages 13 14					$\frac{13\,|\,5}{10\,|\,2}$ −.32	$\frac{10\,|\,8}{7\,|\,5}$ −.06
Exemplification Yes No						$\frac{16\,|\,7}{1\,|\,6}$ +.86
Over-all articles Yes No						

few, more than 13 many. We present the following matrix of fourfold tables and coefficients in our total sample (table 3).

The matrix comes out as we expected. American publications form together with the use of statistics and claim on innovation a cluster, as the three correlations between them are positive; exemplification, over-all articles, high number of references and many pages form another, as all six correlations between them are positive and all their correlations with area, statistics and innovation are negative. This supports our view that articles in USA and Canada tend to value statistics and to claim innovation but pay less attention to exemplification, over-all reviews, many references and pages while articles published in England, France or West Germany show the opposite tendency. This indicates differences in research patterns between our American sample and our European sample.

Are there such differences in the European sample between articles from England and France on the one hand, articles from West Germany on the other? We construct a corresponding matrix for our European sample of 30 articles (table 4).

This matrix suits our summation theory very well, as two clear-cut clusters emerge. The first demonstrates the tendency of statistics, innovation, high numbers of references and many pages to accompany one another and appear more frequently in the Anglo-French articles than in the West German ones. The second is made up only of exemplification and over-all articles, preferred by the West German sociologists.

This indicates that English and French sociologists may differ in research/publication pattern from West German sociologists. But theoretically we would expect that West German researchers, more remote from the United States, not only should rely more on exemplification and over-all reviews but also use more pages and references for their articles. This may, however, be the results of a harder competition for space in the *Kölner Zeitschrift für Soziologie*, than in the French *Archives Européennes de Sociologie*.

Sociologists who accept the American research pattern and stress statistics and innovation are, of course, quite willing to use more pages and to bring in more references in order to elaborate their wiews, but the hard competition for space in American journals does not allow them to do so. They can feel some envy of this European grandeur, but they probably have little wish to take over the European (and especially German) gift for exemplification and over-all reviews. Evidently the West German sociologists in our sample do value these traits and would be surprised to find them challenged. These values are not our values. Still, we must try to interpret them. We believe that German researchers are more concerned with the demarcation lines of their subject, with its legitimate methods, discussions on its theories, eager to demonstrate their ability for penetrating analysis, their fine distinctions, and their wide reading. Values such as these should neither be neglected, nor underestimated.

We ought once more to stress the inadequacy of our samples. It only consists of 41 articles, about the sociology of art. This field is not representative for sociology at large. We do not even know how they do differ from one another.

To us the sociology of art is difficult to formalize and quantify except in some special areas, for example those connected with mass communication and content analysis. This might be one of the reasons why the subject is little appreciated by American researchers. Another could be the small possibilities to apply the results to social or economic advantage; a third the fact that the sociology of art has a comparatively strong position in Europe and in European journals. American specialists in the field should on the one hand try to place their articles in these journals, but on the other are not anxious to do so as they neither rank them high in comparison to the leading American journals, nor are accustomed to their publication policy. All these points explain why we consider our sample adequate in a pilot study on differences in research patterns between American, Anglo-French and West German sociologists.

At last we apply parts of our discussion in the previous chapter to our results. We proposed there that the sociologists' drive for innovation made them less eager to go back to their predecessors and so formed an obstacle for cumulative research, which helped to build communication barriers between researchers in different countries. But there seems to be comparatively little of innovation claims in the sociology of art, yet there are clear-cut differences in research patterns between neighboring countries. We might explain away this contradiction by repeating that the sociology of art is difficult to formalize and quantify. Claims for innovation would then be rare, but other communication barriers between countries would be as cumbersome as in other fields of sociology.

Chapter 5

Time difference in articles on the sociology of alcohol

Charles Snyder and Gunnar Boalt

When we looked for a convenient research field for a small pilot study on changes in sociological problem areas and methods we decided to study the *Quarterly Journal of Studies on Alcohol* for the following reasons:

1. This journal is the principal journal in this field.

2. Its articles are written by researchers representing many sciences, sociology one of them, but by no means dominating.

3. Since 1967 the four numbers of each year contain some 50–60 articles, a convenient number for a small pilot study.

4. We are, both of us, acquainted with this research field and have previously published a content analysis of its main results, Boalt–Jonsson–Snyder: *Alkohol och alienation*, Almqvist & Wiksell, Stockholm 1968, based on the sociological articles in *Quarterly Journal of Studies on Alcohol* from 1957 to March 1967.

5. We suspect that several sociologists in the late 1960's had trouble with the students in their departments and difficulty in adjusting their research projects to a more radical ideology. According to the radical view, alcoholism is to be diagnosed as an illness of society whose cure will result from the revolutionary transformation of society. This outlook made surveys of alcohol behavior appear obsolete.

Sociologists were told their investigations merely enumerated people and behaviors more respectable than themselves. They were accused of defending bourgeois society, of making innocent deviants guilty of anti-social behavior, and of trying to adapt them to an intolerant capitalistic society which should no longer itself be tolerated. We suspect, therefore, that a new generation gap developed about 1967, a gap that ought to show up some years later in published sociological articles. This gap, moreover, should have less effect on the other sciences. Only anthropology would seem as vulnerable as sociology. Anthropologists, after all, are expected to describe and compare societies. And they often felt pressure to use Marxist theory to identify evils and remedies in the societies they studied or lived in.

For these reasons we decided to study the 387 articles published in the years 1965–1972 in the journal and classify them according to:

a) the scientific fields of the articles

b) the type of empirical data presented.

We divided the articles into five fields:

Anthropology. Studies of drinking patterns in cultures, etc.

Sociology. Surveys or studies of special social groups.

Psychology, including social psychology and animal psychology.

Clinical studies on treatment types, etc.

Physiology, including pharmacology and biochemistry.

There is, of course, some overlapping between these fields. When in doubt, we used the following criteria to classify the articles:

1. The kind of department or institution from which the article originated;

2. The department/institution the authors belonged to;

3. The journals (except the *Quarterly Journal of Studies on Alcohol*) most often cited.

Only one article (Vinodorus, by Pierre Grimes) could not be classified.

The most common ways of presenting empirical data were tables and graphs. For our purpose we had little reason to make a distinction, therefore just registering whether there were any of them. Only 87 out of 387 articles did not present quantitative data as tables or graphs.

In comparing the recent articles with earlier ones, we were anxious to classify a substantial number of articles. We believe that the new ideology did not get strong support until 1967, but that it influenced new research first about 1968. The results of this research hardly could be published until 1970. We therefore define recent research as research published in 1970, 1971, and 1972.

Our hypotheses, then, can be set down:

Hypothesis 1. The relative number of sociological articles is higher in 1965–1969 than in 1970–1972.

Table 1. *Number of articles using graphs and/or tables in relation to total number of articles each year 1965–1972 in Quarterly Journal of Studies in Alcohol for five research fields*

Type of field	65	66	67	68	69	70	71	72	Total
Anthropology	0/3	0/3	1/3	1/2	0/1	0/1	1/2	0/0	3/15
Sociology	5/6	4/4	4/4	8/9	3/3	4/7	1/4	5/7	34/44
Psychology	11/14	2/3	9/10	11/14	17/17	15/15	26/27	2/4	93/111
Clinical studies	5/8	9/12	11/19	9/17	13/20	13/17	14/19	12/17	86/129
Physiology	6/6	8/9	11/12	14/15	11/11	13/13	9/9	19/20	91/95
Total	27/37	23/31	36/48	43/57	44/52	45/53	51/61	38/48	300/387

Hypothesis 2. The relative number of anthropological articles is higher in 1965–1969 than in 1970–1972.

Hypothesis 3. The relative number of articles in the fields of psychology, clinical studies and physiology is the same (or a little less) in 1965–1969 as in 1970–1972.

Hypothesis 4. The sociological articles tend to use fewer tables or graphs after 1969.

Hypothesis 5. The articles in clinical psychology, clinical studies and physiology tend to use tables or graphs to the same extent before and after 1969/70.

There is no point in predicting the use of graphs and/or tables in anthropological articles, as they are comparatively few.

We then present for each year and each field the number of articles using graphs and/or tables in relation to the total number of articles (table

Table 2. *Number of articles using graphs and/or tables in relation to total number of articles and as percentages during two periods of Quarterly Journal on Alcohol for five research fields*

Type of field	1965–69	Percent	1970–72	Percent
Anthropology	2/12	17	1/3	33
Sociology	24/26	92	10/18	56
Psychology	50/58	86	43/46	93
Clinical studies	47/76	62	39/53	74
Physiology	50/53	94	41/42	97
Total	173/225	77	134/162	83

1). Let us concentrate these data to the two periods 1965–1969 and 1970–1972 in order to test our hypotheses (table 2).

Hypothesis 1 said that the relative number of sociological articles should be higher in 1965–1969 than in 1970–1972. They are 26/225 versus 18/162, 12% versus 11%. These data hardly support the hypothesis, but point in the right direction.

Hypothesis 2 proclaimed that the relative number of anthropological articles should be higher in 1965–1969 than in 1970–1972. They are 12/225 versus 3/162, 5% versus 2%, which possibly can be said to support the hypothesis.

Hypothesis 3 said that there should be no decrease in the remaining three areas. Psychology changed from 58/225 to 46/162, that is, from 26% to 28%; Clinical studies from 76/225 to 53/162, that is, from 34% to 33% and Physiology from 53/225 to 42/162, that is, from 24% to 26%, which suits the hypothesis well.

Hypothesis 4 predicted that the percent of sociological articles using graphs or tables should decrease after 1969. It goes down from 24/26 to 10/18, from 92% to 56%, showing some support of the hypothesis.

Hypothesis 5 predicted that the percent of articles using graphs or tables should not decrease in psychology, clinical studies and physiology. The percentages change from 86 to 93 in clinical psychology, from 62 to 74 in clinical studies and from 94 to 97 in physiology, thus, supporting the hypothesis.

These data in the main support our view although the sociological articles decreased less than we had expected. However, sociological articles certainly were less quantitative, large-scale surveys disappeared, and the quantitative approach lost its virtual monopoly. In our opinion this indicates a generation gap among sociologists with no corresponding change in sciences less vulnerable to new ideologies.

Does this really mean that sociologists specializing in the alcohol field actually changed research areas or approach? The effect might be the outcome of a new publishing policy in the *Quarterly Journal of Studies on Alcohol.* If so, this change would be just as good an example of short term changes or generation gaps in sociological research publications.

When, finally, we look at the data for each year, the non-quantitative approach appears most pronounced in 1971. Thus we are perhaps already on the way back to quantitative studies. Time will show.

Chapter 6

American schools of sociologists – and Swedish

Gunnar Boalt, Helena Herlin
and Rudy Seward

All sciences have produced their own unique history which can be understood through a selection of its great names, major works, its background, and the social conditions surrounding its research. In an attempt to better understand sociology sociologists can be handled the same way—classified according to status, ideology, theory, problem, method, background, or country. Sorokin, Timasheff and Martindale have already provided us with valuable efforts along these lines by describing the "schools" of sociologists which most sociologists now accept. We accept them too, but at the same time one interesting sociological aspect has been unexplored—these "schools" of sociologists might be thought of as sociological groups which are more or less isolated from one another by communication barriers. Hence their background, communication, norms, and interaction with their colleagues should be studied.

To demonstrate our problem, we have used a grant given by the Swedish Social Science Research Council and the help of Kung Wei Hu, Valerie Malhotra, Terence Russel, Mimi Umana and Otus Vick. Our purpose was to make a study of communication and of the barriers to communication, utilizing citations as an indication of group formation. Our general argument ran something like this: Scientists tend to cite the sources they found useful or impressive during their research, but they sometimes cite scientists in the hope of being reciprocally cited by them. Citing thus indicates similarities in outlook, theory, problem, method, terminology and language or at least a desire for such similarities. Taking a sample of American publications for one year a network of citations could be registered, but the network would be large and difficult to handle plus the resulting groups difficult to label. Hence we decided to use Timasheff's book as a start, listing the authors he cited and classified around 1940. Next taking the four leading sociological journals in 1940—*The American Sociological Review* (handled by Umana), *The American Journal of Sociology* (handled by Kung Wei Hu). *Sociometry* (Russel and Malhotra) and *Social Forces* (Vick)—we extracted all the authors of the articles in the 1940 volumes of these journals. Both the journal authors and Timasheff's authors were ordered alphabetically in one list and all the citations made to these 397 authors' works in the journal articles were registered. We then reduced the number of authors from Timasheff by taking off the list those names not cited in the journal articles. In the same way authors of the articles who were not cited in 1940 by other article writers were dropped from our sample list of cited authors.

This reduced our list to 104 names, a number much easier to handle. We placed all citations into a matrix, the authors of the journal articles (plus additional authors on the list) along the horizontal axis and the cited authors along the vertical axis. Starting with the names most frequently cited—Moreno (16), Burgess (9), Lundberg (8), Chapin, Dewey and Max Weber (7)—we then proceeded to order the names in clusters in such a way as to maximize the citations within each cluster and to minimize citations between clusters. If an author was cited twice, but in two different clusters, we adopted the rule of placing the author in the smaller cluster. Obviously chance considerably influences which cluster a rarely cited name will join.

The outcome was surprisingly simple: only four clusters.

The matrices are reproduced as an Appendix in the end of the book.

The first cluster contained 19 authors, topped by Moreno, Lundberg, Chapin, Dewey, Jennings, Franz, Steele and Dodd; which appropriately could be labelled *Sociometrists and neo-positivists*.

The second cluster had 36 authors, topped by Burgess, W. I. Thomas, Znaniecki, Park, Faris, Frazier, Mowrer and Wirth, all from Chicago. However, authors from other universities were present, for example Read Bain and Cuber (Michigan), and Abel, Alihan, Hankins and Sims (Columbia). In our sample of 104 authors 23 had doctorates from Chicago and 16 of them are included in this cluster. Thus, *The Chicago school* label makes sense, but so does Timasheff's *Human Ecology and Deviance* label.

The third cluster includes only 8 names: Sumner, Linton, Lowie,

Malinowski, Keller, Kluckhohn, Lawsing and Murdock. Their label should be *Social anthropologists* or, in Timasheff's terminology *Functionalists*.

For the fourth cluster containing the remaining authors, we were unable to make several clusters out of its 41 names. Since this cluster is topped by Sorokin, Max Weber, MacIver, Parsons, Mannheim, and Merton, the cluster could be tentatively called *American theoreticians* (including the Europeans accepted by them).

These clusters do not deviate much from Timasheff's classification, but how clearly are the clusters demarcated? The matrix's composition is one answer. A second is comparing the number of citations within the cluster to those outside. This relation is 57/27 for the first cluster, 63/22 for the second, 10/16 for the third, and 78/31 for the fourth, which is a comparatively good result. We believe our method makes sense; however, a number of new problems arise.

The first is the ranking of researchers within the cluster according to citations. Our sample is, of course, too small to say something definite about popularity. Hence we have only used the number of times each author was cited to make the labelling of the clusters easier.

The second problem concerns the background of the cited and citing authors. We have collected some data about them—year of birth, year completed dissertation and year of marriage. Theoretically we expect a young and unknown sociologist to start his career by citing and as his career advances, he is also cited. With further advances in his career, he gets caught in administration etc., which results in his citing less and being cited more, he eventually gives up writing, and finally is cited less and less. We tested this model with our data and got a correlation of -0.29 between age and citing others and a correlation of $+0.08$ between age and citations (by others). If we use year completed dissertation to determine academic age these two correlations (q-coefficients) are $+0.29$ and -0.23 respectively. According to the summation theory, presented by Boalt and Lantz (*The Sociology of Research,* 1969; *Universities and Research*, 1970), we expect married researchers to take the citing game a little less seriously. There is a negative correlation (-0.08) between marriage before 1940 and citing others and a negative correlation (-0.10) between marriage and citation (by others), which means that our hypothesis about the effects of marriage on citing did not stand the test.

The third problem concerns the members of the fourth theoretical cluster. Theorists do cite one another, but in the process of exposing their own theories they often cite others in order to disprove or reject their theories. Thus, using all citations might be misleading in this particular cluster. It should be useful to make a distinction here between positive and negative citations, as the sociometrists distinguish between positive and negative choices. Actually we found 12 cases of negative or critical citations within this cluster. We excluded these citations from the remaining positive ones and tried to form new clusters in which each cluster contained the highest number of positive citations among its members and no negative ones.

The result is three clusters. The first and largest contains 18 authors, among them four classical ones: Weber, Mannheim, Mead, and Pareto. The leading active members are Kingsley Davis, Kirkpatrick, Merton, and Lynn Smith, followed by such names as Hiller, C. Wright Mills, Odum, and Reuter. The number of citations within this large cluster is 29 against 14 outside. Applying Timasheff's terminology this cluster would be labelled the school of *Psychological Sociology*.

The second cluster is smaller with 11 names and only two of them classical: Spencer and von Wiese. The active members are Barnes, Becker, Henderson, MacIver, Parsons, Roethlisberger, Warner, Whelpton and Zimmerman. There are 11 citations within this cluster against 10 outside, which are either to or from the large *Psychological Sociology* cluster. A fusion between these two clusters, however, is prevented by six negative citations between them. Timasheff's label for this second cluster would be *Systematic and Dynamic Sociology*.

The third cluster has 9 names, and two of them—Gurvitsch and Petrazhitsky—are classical and/or European. The dominating names are Sorokin and Timasheff, followed by Hartshorne, Loomis, Taeuber (C. and I.), and Wilson. The 10 citations within the cluster correspond to only 4 citations from outside the cluster. They come from the first cluster and are partly compensated by 2 of the four negative citations. This third cluster thus stands out clearly from the two others. Timasheff seems to have no name for it—maybe because he belonged to it himself.

The fourth problem raises the question: why 1940 and not 1970? We had to test our technique with some kind of control and Timasheff provided this plus the names of authors and labels for our clusters. But we admit the clusters for 1940 seem old-fashioned in 1970. The neo-positivists are now nearly gone, as is the Chicago-school and the social anthropologists have lost most of their importance. Only the theoretical cluster remains, but we suspect it has been split into several new clusters. In labelling these new clusters we can use the subdivisions for the theoretical cluster from 1940, but we dare not use the list of names for our data from 1970—30 years are much too long—hence we try 1955 first. Starting with our list of 104 authors, we added the authors of articles for the same four journals from 1955. This gave us a list of 350 authors, but the citations were more scattered than in 1940. Only 63 authors were cited by the remaining authors, and only three of the classical writers survived.

Matrix 2 is prepared from the citations in the journals for 1955 (or for July 1954 to June 1955, if the volume was arranged this way), using the same techniques as earlier. The result is four clusters. (See Appendix.)

The first consists of 20 names out of Sociometry, starting with Bonney, Moreno, Jennings, Criswell, Northway, Kerr; and ending with Bruner, Chapin, Dewey, Freud, Speroff. These 20 members cite one another 83 times, are cited by other authors 5 times, and cite others only twice. This gives a relation between citations within and those outside the cluster of 83/7. Let us call them *Sociometrists*.

The second cluster contains 25 names, starting with Kingsley Davis, Donald Bogue, Harold Christensen, Harvey Locke, Monahan, Mowrer, Ogburn, Lynn Smith, Wendell Bell, Burgess, Otis Duncan; and ending with Murdock, Redfield, Reiss, Sherif, ... A. Weber. There are 34 citations within the cluster and 5 citations by cluster members of outsiders; thus the relation is 34/5. The cluster includes 7 of the 10 Chicago doctorates in the sample, all the cited anthropologists, ecologists, demonographers, and family sociologists. Despite its disparity it can be labelled *The Chicago school*.

The third cluster is a bit dubious, because most of its 16 names were cited by George Lundberg and/or Theodore Anderson. There are, however, 22 citations within the cluster and 8 outside, thus a 22/8 relation. The list of names starts with Robert Merton, Stuart Dodd, Lazarsfeld, Sorokin, Parsons; and ends with Lundberg, MacIver, McKinney, Dorothy Thomas, Timasheff. The cluster seems to include most of the theorists and could be labelled *The theoretical cluster*.

Finally we have the small cluster or pair, made up of Thomas Ktsanes and Robert Winch who cited one another and thus secure their own membership in a cluster from our list.

Next we observed the background of the citations—their correlations with the characteristics of the citing and the cited authors, for example, year of birth, marital status, etc. We expected citations, given or received, to be related with year of birth. The correlations, however, turned out to be $+0.17$ between age and citations received and $+0.30$ between age and citations of others. If we use year completed dissertation, this academic age is correlated +0.07 with citations received and +0.22 with citations by others. For year of marriage there is a positive correlation with citations received (−0.6), but a negative correlation with citations of others (+0.11).

Dealing with the data from 1969/1970 the same procedures were utilized as with previous data. The original list of authors contained 281 names, out of which only 104 were cited, but when those article authors who were not cited by other authors were excluded only 61 names or 22% remained. The matrix is reproduced in Appendix.

Otis Duncan, cited 14 times, appears to be at the top and center of the first cluster including Blalock (10 citations), Heise (3), Wences (3), Norman Alexander (2), William Sewell (4); and ending with George Lundberg, Sherif, Stouffer, Dorothy Thomas, Weinstein, Harrison White and Zeleny. We could call them *Sociometrists and methodologists*, but the cluster includes authors that do not fit this category, for example, C. Wright Mills. There were 53 citations within the cluster and 18 outside it (53/18).

The second cluster was topped by Robert Merton (12 citations), Wendell Bell (8); and followed by Theodore Newcomb, Kingsley Davis, Paul Lazarsfeld, Eugene Litvak, Arnold Rose, Talcott Parsons, Sorokin, etc. We could call them Theorists, as they seem to form the majority of the cluster. There were 61 citations within it and 20 outside it (61/20).

There may be a small third cluster consisting of Blumer, Burgess, Carlos and MacIver, although it might just as well be united with the second cluster. There are, however, 4 citations within it, 2 outside it (4/2).

Our data about the three samples is compiled in the table on page 54.

We thus find a more well-knit citing system—citing those who cite you and/or being cited by those you cite—in 1955 than in 1940. But the difficulty in attaching labels to the clusters is greater in 1955 than in 1940, and even greater in 1969.

The classical names tend to be cited less after 1940, resulting from the integration of their work into more recent books by modern American sociologists.

We expected from the beginning that age and marriage would make sociologists less eager to cite authors but only age actually shows a tendency in that direction—at least if you measure age from year completed dissertation and not from year of birth.

Summary data for three samples of authors derived from four U.S. sociological journals

	1940	1955	1969–70
Names remaining from original list	104/397	63/350	61/281
Classical names cited	27/397	3/63	1/61
Percent of citations within the clusters	68%	93%	86%
Correlation:			
age–citations received	+.08	+.17	−.03
age–citations given others	−.29	−.24	−.62
year completed dissertation–citations received	−.23	−.31	−.17
year completed dissertation–citations given others	+.29	+.24	+.71
marriage–citations received	−.10	+.37	+.12
marriage–citations given others	−.08	+.07	+.21

Discussion

The differences we have found between our samples of 1940, 1955, and 1969–1970 could simply be due to our method—maybe it is better adapted for the citation system of 1940 than for the later years. Let us, however, trust the method and see what the findings are. We found in 1940 four distinct clusters, fitting well Timasheff's description of (1) sociometrists and neo-positivists, (2) ecologists and criminologists (or Chicago-school), (3) social anthropologists or functionalists and, eventually, (4) theorists. In 1955 there was still a cluster of sociometrists (publishing mainly in *Sociometry*), a diluted Chicago school (including a few surviving anthropologists) and the remaining group of theorists and methodologists, but the clusters' make up and boundaries suggest that the "schools" simply have been dissolved. The rules for theory, methodology or problems and the tradition of citing great scholars' splendid research apparently were no longer taken seriously by the sociologists, as they often cited outsiders—outside of their "school" or specialty. Why? We surmise that in 1955 departments could no longer be dominated by a single school but had to present a balanced curriculum which dictated having a set of scholars covering the important areas of the discipline. Still, some individual sociologists had succeeded in building their "personal empire" of projects, grants and publications (see Boalt and Lantz, *Universities and Research*, Wiley, 1970, pp. 86–95). For these empire builders the citing of others may be viewed as a part of their expansion program, and citations by others may be a way of catching the empire builders attention and insuring co-operation.

The two clusters in the citation matrix from 1969–1970 then could possibly indicate that two kinds of empires are developing: the methodological and the theoretical. We suspect, however, that not even this dividing line will hold for long.

These clusters indicate that American sociologists tend to form specialized groups whose members cite one another more than they cite outsiders. To some extent this picture is due to our method of constructing clusters by combining those who cite one another to a cluster. Also, it is difficult to know what per cent of citations within clusters is needed to prove group formation. A percent clearly above 50 would not be enough, unless the clusters also made sense, that is, agreed with Timasheff's labels.

Citations in the Swedish departments of sociology

We can use our citation matrices to study group formation and later also communication barriers—among Swedish sociologists. There are, however, some difficulties. Swedish sociology is young. Few books and articles were published by Swedish sociologists before 1960 and the number published per year is still comparatively small. To obtain an adequate number of citations we have to take the publications for a number of years and have chosen the period from 1965 to 1971. A period before 1965 would yield too few publications to make a comparison meaningful, as the sociology departments were only in their initial stages of development prior to 1965—chairs in sociology with departments attached to them were created in 1947 at Uppsala University, in 1954 at Stockholm, in 1955 at Lund, in 1960 at Gothenburg, and in 1965 at Umeå. These departments needed time to organize sociological research and to have the results published. Previously the necessary sociological studies had been made by statisticians, economists or even political scientists.

There are no studies of "schools" among Swedish sociologists; however, each department quickly found its own theoretical and methodological style, a style generally imposed and forged by the full professor acting as chairman. When the new generation of sociologists matured, established contacts abroad, and felt secure in their positions, they soon began to follow the pattern of American sociologists or to go back to the pattern of classical European sociologists. But we suspect that they still show a decided tendency to cite their chairman and the established researchers in their own department. In order to identify these department clusters, we always include the full professors in our sample of researchers.

To use our data for comparisons, we had to deal only with material published by Swedish sociologists. As there are reasons to keep articles and books apart, our most convenient comparisons would be between the citation pattern emerging from articles and the pattern emerging from books. Each one should of course show the same principal schools with members citing each other more frequently than citing outsiders.

We have taken our sample of articles by Swedish authors from *The American Journal of Sociology, American Sociological Review,* (although only a few Swedes have been published in these two), *Acta Sociologica,* and *Sociologisk forskning* (these two yielded far more names). To these we added two journals of environmental hygiene: *Archives of Environmental Hygiene* and *Public Health Reports.* Our sample of books included only monographs (not textbooks) and first editions. To provide a sample large enough we had to use a number of years—from 1965 to June 1971. A preliminary report of our results was published in Internat. J. Contemp. Soc. 1971.

The original list of article authors still was rather short and with the elimination of non-professors not citing authors on the list or not cited by these authors, there remained only 27 authors and/or full professors. When authors collaborated on articles, we put both their names—or the first two names if more than two authors—on our list. We end up with 118 articles citing our 27 names 143 times.

Young researchers, of course, seldom write articles, but those who do theoretically should be anxious to cite the authorities in their own department, but still rarely be cited themselves. Once they have made their Ph.D. with honors, they should be cited more and be far more willing to cite professors and experts outside their own department. This altruistic tendency to cross the communication barriers probably results from a very egoistical reason. Young researchers hope for a chair as full professor, which means that their publications are to be evaluated by three full professors. They do not know which professors will be chosen to do the evaluation; hence they are anxious to cite them all if they can find a pretext. But if they are promoted to professors, there is no longer any need for altruism and they should return to the names, the books, the problems that are part of their own more or less isolated departments. Professors usually take on administrative burdens, thus, after a tremen-

Table 1. *Mean number of articles and citations 1965–1971 by four types of researchers*

Mean number of	Researchers not yet Ph.D.	Ph.D. with honors (docenter)	Professors for a part of the period	Full professors for the whole period
Articles	3	4	6	4
Citations made in articles	4	9	5	3
Received citations	2	3	7	13

dous spurt to make a good showing in the competition, they publish less but are cited more and more.

To test these hypotheses we classified our 27 researchers into four groups: researchers without Ph.D. or Ph.D. without honors, Ph.D. with honors (docent), full professors for a part of the period 1965–1971 and then the full professors for the whole period 1965–1971. There are six authors in our sample who have not yet achieved their Ph.D. with honor: Bengt Gesser, Sten Johansson, Dan Jonsson, Jan Lindhagen, Per Sjöstrand, and Håkan Wiberg. The Ph.D.s with honors (docenter) include Bengt Abrahamsson, Johan Asplund, Hans Berglind, Walter Korpi, Karl-Erik Rosengren, Bengt Rundblad and Jan Trost. The professors appointed for a part of the period 1965–1971 are Bo Andersson, Gösta Carlsson, Rune Cederlöf, Ulf Himmelstrand, Joachim Israel, Carl-Gunnar Janson, Erland Jonsson, Georg Karlsson, Harald Swedner and Stefan Sörensen. Then there remains only the four full professors who have been full professors during the entire period: Gunnar Boalt, Edmund Dahlström, Torgny Segerstedt and Hasse Zetterberg. Data about these four groups are presented in table 1.

Table 1 certainly suits our hypotheses very well. The number of articles published reaches a peak among the professors who have been appointed only for a part of the period 1965–1971 and is a little lower among the full professors for the whole period. The citations given in the articles published reaches its maximum among the Ph.D.s hoping to attain a chair, declines among the new professors, and the minimum number is among the full professors. The received citations show a tendency to rise reaching its maximum among the four full professors, enjoying security, status and power to influence the career of the younger researchers.

Status thus seems to be a major determinant of the citation pattern. This raises the question of where the youngest researchers get their citations, as there is little status in citing them—unless their academic advisors are clever enough to stimulate their dissertation work through citations in order to achieve the reputation as successful teachers. These advisors generally belong to our two middle groups as the four full professors in our highest status group publish too little and care too little to show this type of concern. Let us find out. There are 14 citations, citing the researchers who have not yet completed their Ph.D. with honors. Only one of these citations comes from another researcher in the same category, six are from the Ph.D.s with honors, six are from professors holding their appointment only part of the period studied and only one is from the group of four full professors. This evidence supports our contention concerning the citations of young researchers.

In the citation matrix the two names most cited are, very properly, Segerstedt (grand old man of Swedish sociology, received the first chair created in the subject, president of Uppsala University and chairman of the Social science research council) with 22 citations and Boalt (selected as the second professor and during this period dean of the Social science faculty at Stockholm University) honored with 17 citations. Neither one of them had cited other authors on our list but in the citation network they were far apart—authors citing one of these men infrequently cited the other man. They were so far apart and so heavily cited that they formed the centers of two different clusters.

The Segerstedt cluster included Joachim Israel (once researcher at Stockholm, then researcher at Uppsala, later professor at Copenhagen, then Lund and recently professor at Roskilde) with 13 citations and Georg Karlsson (formerly researcher at Uppsala and now professor at Umeå) with 12 citations. Together these two form a subcluster within the Segerstedt cluster.

The Boalt cluster also included a subcluster centered around Erland Jonsson, professor at Stockholm university. A summary of the citations within and between these clusters is presented in table 2.

The Israel subcluster thus cited the Segerstedt cluster (excluding the Israel subcluster) rather frequently but carefully avoided citing the Boalt and the Jonsson clusters. The Segerstedt cluster cited the Israel as well as the Boalt cluster. The Jonsson subcluster was the most isolated and had only a few citations outside its own ranks.

These four clearly demarcated clusters lend themselves to some disagreeable conclusions. They give the impression of an academic duck-

Table 2. *Citations within and between the clusters of article authors and full professors*

| | Citation received by clusters labelled | | | | |
Citations made by	Israel	Segerstedt	Boalt	Jonsson	Sum
Israel subcluster	21	18	1	0	40
Segerstedt cluster	13	26	16	0	55
Boalt cluster	6	7	21	0	34
Jonsson subcluster	0	0	2	12	14
Sum	34	44	40	12	143

pond divided between duck flocks anxious to keep apart—anxious to protect their ranking system and their ideas against "outsiders". Foreigners and foreign ideas can be accepted—as long as their representatives stay home or make only short visits because they frequently result in corresponding honors for their hosts and favorable citations of their publications. This "duck pond" pattern should, we hope, slowly disappear as the younger generation takes over. They seem to have more contacts with one another and co-operate more willingly.

Our "duck pond" pattern is, however, no more than a hypothesis: a nasty hypothesis not to be printed unless it can be tested. There are two chances to test this pattern with our data: observing if the clusters belong to different universities and noting if the clusters also differ in their research fields of endeavor.

The Israel subcluster includes all the Gothenburg sociologists but one—Johan Asplund, who recently moved there from Uppsala, hence most of his citations remain in the Segerstedt cluster. On the other hand Sten Johansson from Uppsala still cited the Israel cluster more than the Segerstedt cluster. In addition Israel himself at this time had a position at the Copenhagen university while Georg Karlsson had a position at Umeå university. This cluster thus can be labelled the Gothenburg, Umeå, Copenhagen cluster as only Asplund from Gothenburg is not included, for reasons given above.

The Segerstedt cluster dominated by Uppsala has sent two fine representatives to the United States—Bo Andersson and Hans Zetterberg. Asplund belongs to this cluster, of course, but so does Håkan Wiberg from Lund.

Citations made

No. Name	Status	Arti-cles	Univer-sity	1	2	3	4	5	6	7	8	9	10	11	12	13	14	15	16	17	18	19	20	21	22	23	24	25	26	27	Cita-tions made
1. Dahlström, Edm.	F.Pr.	8	Gbg	■	1			1	1	1			1		3		2	2													9
2. Israel, Joachim	Pro	11	Cop	2	■			1			2	1			2		1	1													10
3. Johansson, Sten	R	8	Upp		4	■	1		1									3	1												10
4. Jonsson, Dan	R	2	Gbg	1	1		■					1																			2
5. Karlsson, Georg	Pro	3	Um		1	1		■																							2
6. Rundblad, B.	Ph.D.	3	Gbg	1	3				■		1																				4
7. Sjöstrand, Per	R	1	Gbg	1	1					■	1																				3
8. Andersson, Bo	Pro	9	US-Upp					1			■	2																			2
9. Asplund, J.	Ph.D.	6	Gbg			1					1	■	2		2		1	1	1		2	1	1								10
10. Himmelstrand	Pro	5	Upp									1	2	■							1	1	1								5
11. Lindhagen, J.	R	1	Upp										2	■	1						1	1	1								5
12. Segerstedt, T.	F.Pr.	0	Upp												■																0
13. Trost, Jan	Ph.D.	8	Upp	1				8					1		8	■			1		6	1	1								27
14. Wiberg, H.	R	6	L												2	1	■														3
15. Zetterberg, H.	Pro	6	US-Upp	1				1			1		1		2			■	1												3
16. Abrahamsson, B.	Ph.D.	4	St				1					1	1		1	1			■	3	3				2	1					9
17. Berglind, H.	PhD.	2	St		1															■	1				1						2
18. Boalt, G.	F.Pr	1	St																		■										0
19. Carlsson, Gösta	Pro	5	L																	1	1	■									1
20. Gesser, B.	R	1	L																		3		■	2	1						1
21. Janson, C.-G.	Pro	3	St	1																	1	2	1	■							4
22. Korpi, Walter	Ph.D.	4	St								1								2	2	3	1	1		■	1					7
23. Rosengren, K.-E.	Ph.D.	2	L								1			1												■					2
24. Swedner, H.	Ph.D.	5	L	1							1								1		1	1			1		■				8
25. Cederlöf, Rune	Pro	6	St																			1						■	4	1	6
26. Jonsson, Erland	Pro	6	St																									3	■	1	5
27. Sörensen, S.	Pro	2	St																									3		■	3
Citations received				7	13	3	2	12	2	1	6	7	7	22	1	7	4	2	17	2	5	5	3	3	1	0	6	4	2		143

The Boalt cluster includes five Stockholm researchers and four from the University of Lund. The Jonsson subcluster is made up of three Stockholm sociologists.

If we exclude the case of Asplund, all the Swedish sociologists from Gothenburg, Umeå and Copenhagen are included in the Israel subcluster, and all the Uppsala sociologists but one, plus two former Uppsala sociologists now in the USA together with one sociologist from Lund are included in the Segerstedt cluster. The Boalt cluster contains only sociologists from Stockholm and Lund, and the Jonsson subcluster only researchers from Stockholm. Thus there is a strong tendency to form geographically separated groups, and although they include more than one university department they are frequently dominated by one department.

What about the research areas, are they restricted in a similar way? Well, the Jonsson subcluster certainly is. The three members are working in the area of environmental hygiene—studying problems of noise, air pullution, tobacco smoking and alcohol consumption. In this area they have practically a research monopoly although in some cases they cite methodologists.

The Israel subcluster, concentrated at Gothenburg, in a similar way has acquired a research monopoly in the fields of industrial sociology and the sociology of housing. They have, in addition, interest in the theory of sociology and thus reasons to cite other theoreticians, most of whom belong to the Segerstedt cluster.

The Segerstedt cluster has a broader orientation with a general emphasis upon sociological theory, while the Boalt cluster (sad to say) for a long time neglected theory and stressed empirical work. There is, thus, a tendency among the sociological departments to specialize in regard to research areas. We can interpret this specialization as an adaptation resulting from departments with few researchers and limited resources which would not permit them to cover more than a restricted area. But this tendency may indicate a drive for isolation very different from the eagerness of American sociological departments to cover as many of the important research areas as possible in order to present a "well balanced curriculum". We believe that Swedish sociology departments until recently had little regard for the latter idea.

The citation pattern in articles thus gave a rather gloomy picture of Swedish sociology. Maybe books and monographs present something more appealing? Using the same technique to select authors, we obtained 30 names, including all full professors. Seventeen of these

Table 3. *Mean number of books and citations 1965–1971 by four types of researchers*

Mean number of	Researchers not yet Ph.D.	Ph.D. with honors	Professors for a part of the period	Full professors for the whole period
Books	1.4	1.8	1.9	4.6
Citations made there	.3.7	6.6	3.4	3.1
Received citations	4.0	4.1	12.1	20.6

authors also appeared in our sample of authors from the journals; hence we expect that our new sample of authors will display a citation pattern similar to that of the journal authors. The thirty authors made 278 citations. Dividing the authors into the same four classes as previously, there are six authors who had not yet received their Ph.D. with honor (docent)—Kerstin Elmhorn, Robert Eriksson, Bertil Gardell, Eivor Johansson, Bertil Olsson and Kerstin Wiedling—ten authors who had the Ph.D. with honor—Johan Asplund, Hans Berglind, Bengt Börjesson, Magnus Hedberg, Walter Korpi, Agne Lundquist, Bengt Rundblad, Kurt Samuelsson, Jan Trost, and Bo Wärneryd—nine professors who had not held their chairs the whole period between 1965 and 1971—Bo Andersson, Gösta Carlsson, Ulf Himmelstrand, Joachim Israel, Carl-Gunnar Janson, Erland Jonsson, Georg Karlsson, Harald Swedner and Knut Sveri—and five professors who had been full professors all those years —Carin Boalt, Gunnar Boalt, Edmund Dahlström, Torgny Segerstedt and Hans Zetterberg.

We expected that junior researchers—without the Ph.D.—should produce few books, cite a moderate number of authors and receive few citations. The Ph.D.s with honors should write more, cite more and be cited more. The professors holding appointments for a part of the period studied should write still more, but cite less although they receive more citations. Finally the full professors should produce the highest number of books because of their status which almost completely assured publication in Sweden. (They find it far more difficult to use their status for publication in foreign journals.) Full professors should make the least number of citations and receive the highest number of citations. The mean number of citations and books is presented in table 3.

Table 4. *Citations of junior researchers and Ph.D.s with honors by their own and by other professors*

| | Citations made by | |
Citations received by	Their own full professor	Other full professors
Researchers not yet Ph.D. with honor	12	1
Ph.D.s with honor (docent)	7	7

The data do fulfil our expectations. Again, as in our journal sample, the junior researchers got an ample number of citations and we still expect that they received most of them from their academic advisors —from Ph.D.s with honors and from professors for only a part of the period studied. Actually they have only received one citation from their own group, six from the Ph.D.s with honor, four from the professors holding appointments for a part of the period, but thirteen from the full professors. Thus, the full professors occupying a chair during the whole period were far more generous than we had anticipated. We suspect that this generosity is received from the junior researchers' own professors —within the same department—not from other full professors. In addition we can compare the junior researchers with the Ph.D.s with honor in regard to citations received by their own versus other professors, as other professors can be expected to pay far more attention to the latter group. Table 4 provides data for these comparisons.

There is thus a decided tendency among full professors holding chairs during the whole period to cite their own young researchers without the Ph.D. but not those from other departments. This is not only a part of the general isolation pattern, but indicates further isolation at this level as the usual citation clusters often were made up of several departments. Thus for junior researchers there is evidently few chances to receive any attention from full professors outside their own department, not even from professors in allied departments.

As there are three women among the junior researchers, we can compare them with the three men, to see if they give or receive less attention for our four categories of researchers. Female researchers are

Table 5. *Citations given and received by three female and three male junior researchers by type of researcher*

	Citations received or given by			
	Junior researchers	Ph.D.s with honors	Professors	Full professors
Female researchers				
Citing	1	0	17	1
Cited	0	3	4	1
Male researchers				
Citing	0	2	7	8
Cited	0	3	0	12

in Sweden still few in number and considered at least by the older generation of researchers as a bit odd. We expected female researchers to have more in common and identify more with the younger set of professors than with the full professors. Table 5 presents our data. The citations indicate that female researchers seem to have more in common with the younger set of professors—those with appointments only for part of the period from 1965–1971—and less in common with the full professors for the entire period. The male researchers display the opposite tendency. This might reflect the traditional European system of building research empires with a full professor at the top, with his favorite pupil next and followed by a hierarchy of lesser researchers. All members of the research empire were men, all were waiting for their promotion to favorite pupil and all identified themselves with the professor, with this favorite pupil and even with one another. This traditional pattern does not allow access to female researchers and thus cannot be used by them. They find it difficult to identify themselves with an older full professor and probably prefer to work with the younger researchers who are more accustomed to co-operation with girls and women throughout their schooling experience.

Observing the citation matrix for books and monographs (next page), we again get four clusters similar to the clusters derived from articles. The first is dominated by Dahlström with 29 citations, Israel with 20 and Georg Karlsson with 18. This cluster can be labelled the Israel subcluster as it has many citation contacts with the next cluster, dominated by

Citations made in books

	University	1	2	3	4	5	6	7	8	9	10	11	12	13	14	15	16	17	18	19	20	21	22	23	24	25	26	27	28	29	30	Citations made
1. Dahlström, Edmund	Gbg		7	1	4		2	2				2	1															1				18
2. Gardell, Bertil	Gbg	3			4														1													8
3. Hedberg, Magnus	Gbg						1								1																	2
4. Israel, Joachim	Cop	2				2	5	1	1	1		3						1	1									2	1		1	19
5. Johansson, Eivor	Gbg				1								1																			1
6. Karlsson, Georg	Um			1									1																			1
7. Rundblad, Bengt	Gbg			1																												1
8. Andersson, Bo	US												3																			3
9. Asplund, Johan	Gbg	1	1					7				2	1																			12
10. Himmelstrand, Ulf	Upp														5																	0
11. Lundquist, Agne	Gbg											4																				7
12. Segerstedt, Torgny	Upp	1			1						1	1		1				3						1								7
13. Trost, Jan	Upp	1					10				2		11					1	1		1	1	1									33
14. Zetterberg, Hans	US	1											1			1		6	1							1						4
15. Berglind, Hans	St	8	2		1			2	1	1				1	1			3		3	3	3		1	1			1				28
16. Boalt, Carin	L							1										1		1	1	4		1	1							8
17. Boalt, Gunnar	St	3		1	1		3	3			1	1	2	1	1		2	1	3	3	3	9		1	1	1						34
18. Carlsson, Gösta	St	1																3														5
19. Erikson, Robert	St																	2														2
20. Janson, C.-G.	St	2		1														2						1		1			1			8
21. Jonsson, Erland	St							1				1	1	1	1		7				2							1				14
22. Korpi, Walter	St	1			3		1					1	1	1					2	1												13
23. Olsson, Bertil	St	1			1							2	1					1				1										7
24. Samuelsson, Kurt	St	2																	1													3
25. Swedner, Harald	L				1																											2
26. Wiedling, Kerstin	St	1					2	3										1	2			1	1									11
27. Wärneryd, Bo	St	1			2		2	2					1					1	1		2	2										10
28. Börjesson, Bengt	St																												3	5		9
29. Elmhorn, Kerstin	St																													4		7
30. Sveri, Knut	St																		1									1	2		1	1
Citations received		29	9	4	20	3	18	12	7	2	5	10	31	2	8	1	4	31	12	4	15	19	1	3	3	3	1	5	2	4	10	278

Table 6. *Citations within and between the clusters of book authors*

| Citations made by | Citations received by clusters labelled | | | | |
	Israel	Segerstedt	Boalt	Sveri	Sum
Israel subcluster	33	9	6	2	50
Segerstedt cluster	18	32	17	0	67
Boalt cluster	44	24	76	1	145
Sveri subcluster	0	0	3	13	16
Sum	95	65	99	16	278

Segerstedt with 31 citations. The third cluster still can be labelled the Boalt cluster which he dominates with 31 citations. In the Boalt cluster there is a subcluster dominated by Professor Knut Sveri, criminologist at Stockholm University, which will be labelled the Sveri subcluster.

We can sum up the citations from the matrix in table 6. All four clusters show, of course, a strong tendency to cite their own members. The Sveri subcluster seems to be the most exclusive one.

The four clusters emerging from the book citations appear to show the same pattern as that from the article matrix. But books provide far better chances for citations than articles. There was a mean of 9.3 citations for our authors per book but only a mean of 5.9 per article.

Books were often dissertations as all dissertations in Sweden until recently had to be printed before a candidate was granted the Ph.D. Also a book generally gave more status to the author than an article. On the other hand, professors and other researchers with high status generally had little difficulty these years getting their books published. In 1971 the publishers, however, encountered a financial crisis, and getting work published now is far more difficult. But during the period studied these restrictions had not yet appeared. We then expect that authors of books generally had higher academic status than authors of articles, although the highest status should belong to the authors who had published both books and articles. We can test this hypothesis with the data presented in table 7.

Our hypothesis does stand the test, but the difference between authors of books and authors of articles is rather small.

There are two further hypotheses to be tested in regard to our main theme—the isolation tendency of Swedish sociologists. We have tried to explain this tendency not only as ambition and a need to give recognition

Table 8. *Academic status of authors of articles and books, only books, and only articles*

	Researchers not yet Ph.D. (1)	Ph.D. with honors (2)	Professors but not the whole period (3)	Professors the whole period (4)	Mean rank
Authors of cited books and articles	0	5	7	4	3.0
Authors only of cited books	6	5	1	2	1.9
Authors only of cited articles	6	2	3	0	1.7

to one's own research reference group—friends, advisors and professors —but further as an expression of this same group's influence on research problems, theories and methods. This tendency should, however, be counteracted by a tendency among the qualified Ph.D.s with honors seeking a chair anxiously citing all full professors, who might determine their qualification for a chair. But professors once they have been granted their chair quickly switch back to their old affiliations and their old set of problems, methods and theories. The old full professors—professor before 1965—had little reason to cite outsiders. Those holding Ph.D.s with honor thus should scatter their citations over all clusters and should be especially anxious to cite the Swedish full professors outside their own department. We can test this hypothesis for all citations, from articles as well as from books, for our four categories of sociologists with the data presented in table 8.

For each category we computed a measure of loyalty to one's own cluster as Q-coefficients between belonging to a cluster and citing it.

	Correlation
Sociologists not yet Ph.D. with honor	+.81
Ph.D.s with honors	+.54
Professors during part of period 1965–1971	+.86
Full professors during the whole period 1965–1971	+.86

Ph.D.s with honors had, as we expected, a lower correlation and were more willing to cite outside their own cluster. This generosity seems to disappear for those who have been appointed professors.

The Ph.D.s should in particular be willing to cite Swedish full professors. We can test this second hypothesis by examining the sociologists

Table 9. *Citations from the Segerstedt cluster and the Boalt cluster made by their members*

	Citing	
	Segerstedt cluster	Boalt cluster
Not yet Ph.D. with honor belonging to cluster		
Segerstedt	27	11
Boalt	5	19
Ph.D.s with honors belong to cluster		
Segerstedt	72	40
Boalt	23	43
Professors, not whole period, belonging to cluster		
Segerstedt	35	15
Boalt	7	41
Professors, whole period belonging to cluster		
Segerstedt	35	13
Boalt	6	29

citing Carin Boalt, Gunnar Boalt, Edmund Dahlström and Torgny Segerstedt. The data are presented in table 10.

The Ph.D.s with honors evidently have the strongest tendency to cite Swedish full professors outside their own department. We interpret this as an attempt to influence potential experts who will evaluate their production when they apply for a chair.

The fact that no full professors cited other full professors at the same department has a very simple explanation: no department had more than one full professor holding this appointment during the whole period 1965–71.

Table 10. *Academic status of authors citing Swedish full professors holding chairs 1965–1971*

Sociologist belonging to	Sociologists not yet Ph.D. with honor (1)	Ph.D. with honors (docent) (2)	Professors but not the whole period (3)	Professors the whole period (4)
The professor's own department	11	12	12	0
Other departments	2	31	14	13

Discussion of previous findings

We now turn to the problem of communication barriers demonstrated by the citation matrices in sociological publications. This restriction to sociology implicitly takes for granted, that we expect sociologists to pay little attention—and few citations—to researchers in other fields. Then we must admit, explicitly, that citations may in the same way be restricted to special fields in sociology. That is, we accept specialization barriers between different periods or different regions. This is easy to say and difficult to do, as "unpermitted" differences between periods or regions are more or less bound up with "acceptable" differences in special fields, but to what degree generally is difficult to ascertain. All we can do is to discuss each case, using the information we have. And so, let us review our citation matrices once more, looking for barriers against scientific communication.

Our first matrix, from United States in 1940, had four clusters representing four research fields. One of the fields, "Human ecology and Deviance" is, however, also labelled "the Chicago school" as it includes so many sociologists, active or trained there: E. Burgess, W. I. Thomas, F. Znaniecki, R. Park, E. Faris, F. Frazier, E. Mowrer, L. Wirth, Nels Anderson, W. Ogburn et al. Our sample contained 104 authors, 23 of them graduated from Chicago and 16 of these included in the cluster. This might indicate a barrier against communication between Chicago and other universities, possibly strengthened by the high status of the Chicago department at this time. If so, this cluster (the second in matrix 1) should cite their own members more frequently than the other clusters do cite theirs.

In order to test these ideas we summarize matrix 1 in the following table:

| Citations received in | Citations given by | | | |
	Cluster 1	Cluster 2	Cluster 3	Cluster 4
Cluster 1 (sociometrists and neo-positivists)	57	4	1	11
Cluster 2 (the Chicago school)	3	63	0	5
Cluster 3 (social anthropologists)	0	3	8	1
Cluster 4 (American theorists)	8	6	0	80

We measured the isolation tendency within each cluster as the relation between citations given within the cluster and the total number of citations given or received by members of the cluster. Cluster 1, sociometrists and neo-positivists, then had 57/84=68% of the citations exchanged between the members; cluster 2, the Chicago-school, had 63/85=74%; cluster 3, the social anthropologists, had 10/16=62% and cluster 4, American theorists, had 78/109=71%. The mean tendency was 208/294=71%. This might be taken as a rather weak support to our expectation that the Chicago-school in 1940 still had a slight tendency to regional isolation.

Did this tendency in the Chicago school still survive in 1955? The matrix contained 63 sociologists. Ten of them had graduated in Chicago and seven of these belonged to cluster 2. Seven sociologists worked at Chicago University and six of them belonged to cluster 2, and so it was labelled the Chicago-school. We prepared a table corresponding to the previous one:

Citations received	Citations given by			
	Cluster 1	Cluster 2	Cluster 3	Cluster 4
Cluster 1 (sociometrists)	83	1	2	1
Cluster 2 (Chicago-school)	0	34	0	0
Cluster 3 (American theorists)	2	3	22	0
Cluster 4 (Ktsanes and Winch)	0	0	0	2

We computed the isolation tendency within each cluster in the same way. Cluster 1 (sociometrists) had 83 citations within the cluster out of 89, that is, 93%, cluster 2 (the Chicago school) had 34 out of 38 for 89%, cluster 3 (American theorists) 22 out of 29 for 76% and the small Ktsanes–Winch cluster 2 out of 3. The mean of the whole matrix was 89% (141/159). The second cluster, including the Chicago-school was, thus, not more isolated or specialized than the mean, and so there should be no regional barrier against communication. On the other hand the sociologists at Chicago still might be more isolated than the other members of the cluster. Well, we could pick out the 13 sociologists, who had graduated from Chicago or who worked there in 1955 and compare their citations with the remaining 50. This gave us our next table:

| | Citations given by | |
Citations received by	13 Chicago men	50 others
13 Chicago men	6	12
50 others	13	128

The Chicago men evidently had a strong tendency to cite one another. Yes, but this might be the outcome of their concentration in cluster 2, where they are expected to cite others from cluster 2. Actually all six citations of Chicago men by Chicago men were from cluster 2 to cluster 2. This fact has cleared them definitely from suspicions of creating barriers against scientific communications.

What about the matrix of 1969–70? There were 61 sociologists divided among three clusters. Twelve sociologists had taken their doctorate's degree in Chicago; six of them belonged to cluster 1, four to cluster 2, and two to cluster 3. It is no longer possible to speak of a Chicago cluster. Still, Chicago men may have a tendency to prefer one another. We construct the following table:

| | Citations given by | |
Citations received by	20 Chicago men	41 others
20 Chicago men	14	31
41 others	22	69

The 20 Chicago men had a very weak tendency to cite each other, but of the fourteen cases where they did so, eleven were in the same cluster, only three were not. There was evidently no signs of communication barriers.

Our American materials thus gave a slight indication of communication barriers in 1940, but no indications in 1955 or in 1969–1970. We now turn back to our Swedish materials, and have no difficulty at all to point out strong communication barriers between the sociological departments: Uppsala, Gothenburg and Umeå more or less united, more or less isolated from Stockholm and Lund, which formed another part of the "duck pond".

The Swedish material also demonstrated the strong dominance of a few full professors, cited very often but not very generous themselves in citing others. Peculiar generation gaps also complicated the picture, but made sense if they were seen as parts of the "duck pond" pattern. Young researchers, not yet Ph.D., but able to publish, had of course few books, cited rather few researchers, but honored especially the full professor of their own department. Once they had made a good thesis, they started to cite also full professors from other departments, which might be due to their wish for a professor's chair; this chair available only after a thorough evaluation made by three full professors, and so these were handled very respectfully by aspiring candidates. As soon as a candidate is appointed full professor, he tends to return to his old citation habits, including some of his new disciples among those he takes the trouble to cite. Female researchers evidently found some kind of barrier between themselves and the old full professors, but they cited and were cited by the younger researchers, who evidently found it easier to communicate with them.

All these communication barriers belong to a pattern probably taken over from the Central European universities as they flourished before World War I. The professor dominated, or rather, *was* the department. His disciples were his property, earmarked, and hardly welcome at another university. They formed a hierarchy, from the favorite at the top, next to the professor, down to the freshmen. Loyalty was not only important for good marks but also for one's career, since the favorite of a good professor stood a good chance to get a chair himself—as the professor would consider this a compliment to himself and his "school", a chance to expand his empire and a blow to his silly competitors.

In this way the academic duck pond was divided between a number of drakes, each followed by his batch of faithful ducklings. When they grew a little bigger, they found, however, there were more drakes than their own in the pond and they immediately paid them respect—until they were promoted to plumage and rank of drake themselves. Female ducks were misplaced in the pond.

This pattern was hardly accepted in England, but we guess that many American scholars brought some of it into the United States. Possibly the Chicago school in 1940 had some remnants of it. But otherwise American universities had a highly mobile staff, expanded so quickly and were so eager to present a balanced curriculum that the communication barriers were swept away. It is our impression that the barriers after all are shrinking even in Sweden.

Chapter 7

Researchers and teachers at a sociological department

Arne Bjurman

My population of researchers consists of 67 sociologists who had gained their M.A. at the university of Stockholm before 1973. Six of the variables used to characterize them and their M.A. theses are taken from official data, but twelve others were estimated by me and Gunnar Boalt. The reliability of these estimations is computed by comparing my and Boalt's estimations of the 37 cases known to both of us. Our estimations are, though, not quite independent. We have not discussed our estimations, but each department tends to reach a consensus on the researchers' and their theses' merits and weaknesses. Several of these theses go back in time more than twenty years and some of the traits we estimated, for instance ego strength, are demonstrated under rather special conditions, not always open to outsiders. Some traits will then get a rather low reliability and yet give valuable information. One of the traits, no. 10, status among students, could, however, be used only for those researchers working as teachers at the department in 1972 and had to be excluded from the study of researchers. The traits 1–9, 11–12 were all of them estimated by Boalt with five-point scales; one point given to 8 researchers, two points given to 15, three to 21, four to 15 and five to 8. I have given the 37 cases known to me the corresponding distribution. Five-point scales were used also for traits 13 and 14, but the traits 15–18 only dichotomized.

The researchers' traits were defined this way:
1. Ego strength. Ability to retain balance and reality contact under severe stress. Reliability +0.39.

2. Independence in choice of subject for thesis, especially independence of the professor. Reliability +0.45.
3. Independence in method. Ability to find new approaches. Reliability +0.40.
4. Perseverance. Ability to keep difficulties present, until they can be well handled. Reliability +0.42.
5. Level of aspiration for theory in thesis. Reliability +0.50.
6. Level of aspiration for methods in thesis. Reliability +0.39.
7. Ability for innovations in theory and method. Reliability +0.61.
8. Status outside the department (for instance in civil service, mass media). Reliability +0.62.
9. Status in peer-group at the department. Reliability +0.65.
11. Status among professors. Reliability +0.55.
12. Personal contact with professor. Reliability +0.55.
13. Marks in M.A. 1. Low mark, 2. Medium, 3. High mark, 4. Ph.D., 5. Professor.
14. Printed production. 1. None, 2. Some at a low level, 3. Popular science, article(s) in journals or part of a book, 4. Restricted production at a high level, 5. Large production at high level.
15. Sex. As we suspect female sex is a drawback, we classify 1. Females, 2. Males.
16. Choice of career. 1. Giving up research, 2. Going on with research.
17. Appointment at some Swedish Sociology Department. 1. No, 2. Yes.
18. Appointment at the Sociology Department in Stockholm. 1. No, 2. Yes.
30. Employment at the Sociology Dept. in Stockholm during 1972. 1. No, 2. Yes. Used later.

The reliability data are computed as product moment coefficients, and so are the correlations between the variables 1–9, 11–14. All correlations with the variables 15–18 are computed as Q-coefficients. I use these correlations to study the interaction between the traits as they looked from Boalt's point of view at the time of the researchers' M.A. graduation. I admit that he up to a point may have been influenced by their later performances. This halo effect is hardly possible to avoid, but should neither be ignored nor forgotten by the careful reader.

The correlations are presented in matrix 1, page 76. It demonstrates a number of interesting points. The academic career traits (variables 13, 14, 16, 17 and 18) are highly correlated with one another and with status (variables 8, 9 and 11), methods (6), independence (2 and 3), innovation

(7) and male sex (15). Ego strength (1), perseverance (4), level of aspiration, theory (5) and personal contact with the professor (12) seem to be of less importance to status and career.

The level of aspiration to method, thus, seems to be more important to status and career than the level of aspiration to theory. Why? Researchers are, after all, better rewarded for an elegant theory than for a well drilled methodology. Yes, possibly now, but not formerly at this department. In order to test my hunch, that there is a recent change in the research policy concerning the formerly less appreciated traits 1, 4, 5 and 12, I divide my material in five period groups:

1. M.A. examination prior to 1954. The pioneers. 13 cases.
2. M.A. examination 1955–1959. 13 cases.
3. M.A. examination 1960–1964. 14 cases.
4. M.A. examination 1965–1968. 14 cases.
5. M.A. examination after 1968. 13 cases.

The first group, the 13 pioneers, gained their M.A. before there was a Chair in Sociology at the Stockholm University, although the research area was so attractive that a number of young men were allowed to take their M.A. or Ph.D. in it. Some of these produced sociological research and, as they had an early start, have been appointed full professors. The next group gained their M.A. at a time when the university had created a university department of Sociology—employing only pioneers. As the department grew, more assistants and lecturers were needed. But the student unrest and a new ideology led to changes in teaching and research, changes which could not influence the M.A. theses until in 1969.

In order to compare researchers from the five different periods I compute the means of the first 14 variables in each period and present them in the table on page 77.

The pioneers, graduated before 1954, appear as a superior group from most aspects and have a mean of 3.6. The next group, graduated between 1955 and 1959, is far lower and its mean as low as 2.6, indicating that the new-fangled department was scarcely attractive and/or unable to promote good research. The next period, 1960–1964, gave a better yield, with a mean of 3.0. The two last periods came very near, with means of 2.8 and 2.9. But the superiority of the pioneer group to some extent depends on the fact that the pioneers have had more time for promotion (variable 13) and printed production (variable 14). If we exclude these two variables, the mean of the pioneers does, however, not drop very much, only from 3.6 to 3.5.

Matrix 1. Correlations from a population of 67 sociologists with M.A. from the university of Stockholm

Variables	1	2	3	4	5	6	7	8	9	11	12	13	14	15	16	17	18	30
1. Ego strength	■	+.13	+.10	+.25	+.18	+.04	+.33	+.33	+.20	+.30	+.67	-.05	+.10	-.14	+.28	+.42	-.04	+.28
2. Independence in subject		■	+.52	+.33	+.40	+.30	+.62	+.40	+.45	+.41	+.15	+.54	+.67	+.14	+.77	+.55	-.04	+.07
3. Independence in method			■	+.50	+.50	+.41	+.71	+.47	+.55	+.59	+.36	+.58	+.55	+.29	+.80	+.63	+.15	+.28
4. Perseverance				■	+.70	+.51	+.73	+.31	+.63	+.59	+.36	+.42	+.48	+.29	+.92	+.71	-.50	+.40
5. Level of aspiration. Theory.					■	+.25	+.58	+.14	+.43	+.48	+.23	+.43	+.26	+.14	+.51	+.55	+.61	+.40
6. Level of aspiration. Method.						■	+.59	+.38	+.43	+.48	+.23	+.43	+.26	+.36	+.83	+.71	+.61	+.51
7. Innovation							■	+.59	+.38	+.79	+.36	+.61	+.36	+.43	+.95	+.71	+.61	+.51
8. Status outside department								■	+.58	+.75	+.33	+.51	+.55	+.66	+.88	+.79	+.50	+.51
9. Status in peer-group									■	+.83	+.33	+.52	+.59	+.71	+.92	+.84	+.26	+.51
11. Status among professors										■	+.86	+.72	+.62	+.66	+.83	+.84	+.79	+.51
12. Personal contact with professor											■	+.66	+.52	+.43	+.51	+.93	+.75	+.61
13. Marks in M.A. etc.												■	+.56	+.35	+.66	+.71	+.61	+.40
14. Printed production													■	+.72	+.98	+.85	+.41	-.21
15. Sex														■	+.82	+.79	+.26	+.07
16. Choice of career															+1	+.63	+.42	+.63
17. Appointment at some sociol.dep.																+1	+.78	+.25
18. Appointment at Stockholm sociol.dep.																	+1	+.90
30. Employment at Stockholm sociol.dep. in 1972																		+1

Table 1. *Arithmetic means of researchers' variables in M.A.s during 5 periods of time*

Variables	Arithmetic means of variables during the period				
	−1953	1954–59	1960–64	1965–68	1969–
1. Ego strength	2.9	2.7	3.4	2.9	3.2
2. Independence in choice of subject	3.8	3.0	2.9	2.5	2.8
3. Independence in method	3.6	2.7	2.8	2.9	3.0
4. Perseverance	3.5	2.5	3.0	2.6	3.4
5. Level of aspiration. Theory	3.2	2.5	2.9	2.6	3.7
6. Level of aspiration. Method	3.5	2.4	3.1	3.0	2.9
7. Innovation	3.8	2.5	3.2	2.6	2.9
8. Status outside the department	3.6	2.5	3.5	2.9	2.5
9. Status in peer-group	3.7	2.5	2.9	2.6	3.1
11. Status among professors	3.7	2.5	3.2	2.9	2.9
12. Personal contact with professor	3.2	2.8	2.6	2.8	3.4
13. Marks in M.A., etc.	3.7	2.8	2.9	3.1	2.7
14. Printed production	4.1	2.4	3.1	2.8	2.4
Mean of variables 1–14	3.6	2.6	3.0	2.8	2.9
Mean of variables 1–12	3.5	2.6	3.0	2.8	3.0
Number of cases	13	13	14	14	13
Number of women	1	4	4	5	4

I expected that the researchers from the period after 1968, exposed to a new research ideology would pay more attention to theory than previous researchers and also tend to have more ego strength (1), perseverance (4) and personal contact with the professor (12). Actually the period after 1968 has the highest mean of variable 5, far above any other period and also the highest mean of variable 12. The means of the variables 1 and 4 are not the highest, but next to it. Evidently, there was something in my hunch that the research policy changed after 1968, at least in regard to these four aspects.

The table above stresses the superiority of the 13 pioneers. But were they really as excellent as that? Boalt belonged to them himself and I suspect that he is the victim of a halo effect: knowing them well and a friend of them, he might have overrated them. This is, however, not easy to prove. One possibility is to compare Boalt's estimations with my own of the 37 cases both of us have estimated. This gives the table on page 78.

Table 2. *Mean differences between Boalt's and my own estimations of researchers' variables during 5 periods of time*

Variables	Arithmetic means of differences during the period				
	−1953	1954–59	1960–64	1965–68	1969–
1. Ego strength	−1.0	−0.2	−0.1	+0.6	±0
2. Independence in choice of subject	±0	+0.2	−0.4	+0.4	−0.3
3. Independence in method	−0.3	+0.4	±0	−0.1	−0.5
4. Perseverance	−0.7	−0.4	±0	+0.1	−0.7
5. Level of aspiration. Theory	−0.3	−0.6	−0.1	+0.4	−0.5
6. Level of aspiration. Method	−1.0	−0.2	−1.1	−0.4	−0.3
7. Innovation	−0.3	−0.6	−0.3	±0	−0.1
8. Status outside the department	+0.7	−0.2	+0.1	±0	+0.1
9. Status in peer-group	−1.3	−1.2	−0.5	+0.2	±0
11. Status among professors	−1.0	−1.0	−0.6	+0.7	−0.1
12. Personal contact with professor	−1.0	−0.8	−0.6	+0.1	+0.5
Mean of variables	−0.6	−0.4	−0.3	+0.1	−0.2
Number of persons in period	3	5	8	9	12

My own estimations generally tend to be lower than Boalt's for a very simple reason: I have no impressions of 30 researchers because they have left the department. They generally left because they were not very good researchers. My population then is better than Boalt's, but we use the same scales and same distribution of points. My points then tend to be lower than Boalt's. But Boalt and I disagree most on the pioneers, and so Boalt may up to a point be the victim of a halo effect. On the other hand the pioneers may be a good group for the simple reason that it included only one woman. See table 1.

If Boalt overrated his own peer-group, I myself may have done so too. I belong to the period 1965–68 and that period is the only one where my estimations slightly exceed those of Boalt. I am afraid both of us have overrated our own peer-groups.

I sum up these data on the researchers' production and career:

1. The status and the reputation of the subject affect the selection and the production of its candidates. A department in being attracts good students hoping to be employed and to influence the framing of the new subject. The pioneers (before 1954) differ considerably from the candidates in the established department (1954–59).

2. The curriculum rewards certain types of abilities. The raised level of aspiration for theory in the period after 1968 is a good example.
3. The professor probably affects the recruiting to the department, the marks given in examinations and the resource allocation to research. This is demonstrated in the correlations between personal contacts, marks and career. But the professor seems to have less influence on the printed production.
4. I expected ego strength (1) to affect production and career considerably as it might counteract the strangling effect of perfectionism. Somehow, this effect is not visible in the matrix. Innovation (7) on the other hand seems to be very important as it unites (or consists of) independence (2, 3), perseverance (4), level of aspiration (5, 6) and status (8, 9, 11): all of them correlated with academic career and printed production (13, 14). I can, alas, not carry my analysis further than the matrix allows. Boalt and Bohm have, however, done so, using the "summation theory" as it is presented in Boalt–Lantz–Ribbing: *Resources and Production of University Departments: Sweden and U.S. (Stockholm 1972)*.

I now leave the 67 researchers and turn to the 26 of them who were employed as teachers at the department in 1972. My first step is to compare them with the 41 not employed at the department. In order to do so I introduce a new variable: no. 30: Employment at the department in 1972, very similar to variable 18: Appointment at the Sociology Department in Stockholm, but not identical with it as no. 18 pertains to permanent employment but no. 30 also includes temporary employment.

The correlations of variable 30 in matrix 1, page 76, with the other variables indicate, that the teachers employed in 1972 generally had lower research merits than those who had been appointed professors. It is evident that they were below the general standard in marks (variable 13), as the correlation is -0.21. This does not mean, that low marks represent a kind of merit for employment. I believe that good teachers often gave too much time and interest to their teaching and so just tried to pass the M.A. examination, not caring for honors degrees. And the M.A. was important to them, as they could claim more pay and teach at higher levels, once they had got it, whether they had high or low marks.

The 26 teachers with M.A. employed during 1972, thus, seem to vary considerably in research merits and printed production but on the other hand poor teachers at this time probably had had time to find other work, better suited to them.

In order to study the 26 teachers and their teaching we need a number of traits, taken from registers or estimated. The 18 researchers' traits are available, but to them are added twelve teachers' traits, eight of them estimated by Kerstin Bohm and by myself:

19. Employment at the department in 1972. Applies to all 26, and so is useless here.
20. Academic level of teaching. 1. 1–2 point level, 2. Higher levels.
21. Ability to teach. 1. Low, 2. High. Reliability +0.97.
22. Level of aspiration for the students' results. Reliability +0.30.
23. Radicalism in opinion on society. 1. No, 2. Yes. Reliability +0.97.
24. Level of aspiration for own teaching. 1. Low, 2. High. Reliability +0.84.
25. Preference for type of own teaching. 1. Group discussion, 2. Lecture. Reliability −0.15.
26. Production of teaching material (for instance, stencilled sheets or Xerox). 1. No, 2. Yes. Reliability +0.67.
27. Interest in teaching. 1. Low, 2. High. Reliability +0.84.
28. Interest in theoretical items. 1. Low, 2. High. Reliability +0.84.
29. Years at the department.

In this population variables 17 and 18 come out identical and so variable 17 is excluded. Variable 19 is useless in this case and is also excluded. Variables 22 and 25 are excluded as their reliability, computed as a comparison between my own and Kerstin Bohm's estimations, is too low. Sex (variable 15) is excluded as there are only 3 female teachers among the 26. All correlations are computed as Yule's Q-coefficients. The variables 1–12 are characterized as researchers' traits, 13–19 as career traits and 20–29 as teachers' traits. The correlations between the traits among the 26 teachers with M.A., estimated by myself, are presented in matrix 2, page 81 and estimated by Kerstin Bohm (variables 10, 21, 23, 24, 26–28) in matrix 3, page 82.

I have built my hypotheses on the summation theory, presented in the previous chapters (and in the following chapter, too). If my population of 26 teachers had been a random sample of 67 researchers, the correlations in the matrices 2 and 3 would be dominated by the good teachers with an abundance of good traits and by the poor teachers with bad traits. This would result in a matrix nearly completely made up of positive correlation, just like matrix 1, page 76. But actually the poor teachers either gave up teaching or the department gave up them. The dispersion in teaching

Matrix 2. *Correlations from a population of 26 teachers at the Sociology department in 1972, traits estimated by Bjurman*

Variables	2	3	4	5	6	7	8	9	10	11	12	13	14	16	18	20	21	23	24	27	28	26	29
1. Ego strength	+.54	+.76	+.56	+.85	+.27	+.68	+.65	+.80	+.93	+.85	+.40	+.40	+.53	+.56	+.66	+.33	+.95	+.68	+.45	+.68	+.45	+.45	+.16
2. Independence subject	■	+.90	+.43	+.32	+.32	+.59	+.90	+.50	+.32	+.59	-.20	+.93	+.93	+.85	+.62	+.59	-.32	0	0	-.32	±0	-.59	±0
3. Independence method		■	+.89	+.68	+.68	+.89	+.93	+.60	+.68	+.90	-.02	+.90	+.90	+.89	+.84	+.65	+.16	+.45	+.45	+.56	+.45	-.15	+.45
4. Perseverance			■	+.57	+.57	+.97	+.97	+.76	+.76	+.93	+.43	+.89	+.85	+.93	+.99	+.99	+.57	+.57	+.47	+.56	+.30	-.30	±0
5. Level of asp. Theory				■	+.44	+.67	+.83	+.76	+.97	+.83	+.15	+.44	+.80	+.85	+.16	+.67	+.44	+.93	+.43	+.67	+.67	+.54	-.44
6. Level of asp. Method					■	+.44	+.45	+.76	+.67	+.15	-.30	0	+.80	+.30	+.73	+.84	+.84	+.15	+.15	+.15	+.15	-.15	-.15
7. Innovation						■	+.94	+.68	+.76	+.93	0	+.93	+.93	+.99	+.95	+.99	+.15	+.44	-.45	-.56	+.15	+.15	+.15
8. Status outside department							■	+.86	+.98	+.67	-.02	+.93	+.93	+.99	+.87	+.84	+.22	+.16	-.16	+.30	+.15	-.45	-.16
9. Status in peer-group								■	+.60	+.38	+.45	+.98	+.98	+.97	+.17	+.98	+.32	+.57	+.30	+.56	+.30	-.30	-.30
10. Status among students									■	+.80	+.85	+.85	+.91	+.30	+.90	+.17	+.84	+.92	+.67	+.56	+.15	+.54	-.15
11. Status among professors										■	+.76	+.67	+.32	+.89	+.28	+.84	+.44	+.15	+.43	+.30	-.15	-.30	+.66
12. Personal contact with professor											■	+.57	+.80	+.07	+.96	0	+.30	+.57	-.30	-.30	-.68	-.30	±0
13. Marks in M.A., etc.												■	+.43	+1	+.97	+.93	-.43	0	-.32	±0	+.32	-.80	-.19
14. Printed production													■	+1	+1	+.93	+.93	-.43	0	±0	+.32	-.80	-.30
16. Choice of career														■	+1	+.28	0	-.32	0	+.36	+.30	-.57	±0
18. Appointment of the department															■	+.96	+.15	+.17	+.47	+.48	+.18	-.48	+.17
20. Academic level of teaching																■	+1	+.44	+.15	+.55	+.16	-.48	-.15
21. Ability to teach																	■	+.44	+.67	+.55	-.15	+.67	-.44
23. Radicalism																		■	-.15	+.67	+.83	+.15	+.15
24. Level of aspiration for own teaching																			■	+.15	-.45	+.83	+.15
27. Interest in teaching																				■	+.97	-.67	+.15
28. Interest in theoretical items																					■	+.15	+.15
26. Production of teaching material																						■	-.43
29. Years at the department																							■

Matrix 3. Correlations from a population of 26 teachers at the Sociology department in 1972, traits estimated by Kerstin Bohm

Variables	2	3	4	5	6	7	8	9	10	11	12	13	14	16	19	20	21	23	24	26	27	28	29
1. Ego strength	+.54	+.76	+.56	+.85	+.27	+.68	+.65	+.80	+.85	+.85	+.40	+.40	+.53	+.56	+.66	+.33	+.85	+.68	+.68	+.68	+.85	+.45	+.16
2. Independence, subject	■	+.90	+.43	+.32	+.32	+.59	+.90	+.50	+.33	+.59	−.20	+.93	+.93	+.85	+.62	+.59	±0	−.33	−.33	±0	−.33	±0	±.10
3. Independence, method		■	+.89	+.68	+.68	+.89	+.93	+.60	+.68	+.90	−.02	+.90	+.90	+.89	+.84	+.65	+.68	+.15	+.15	+.68	+.15	+.45	+.15
4. Perseverance			■	+.57	+.76	+.97	+.83	+.84	+.76	+.93	+.43	+.89	+.85	+.93	+.99	+.99	+.57	+.57	+.57	+.57	+.30	+.30	±0
5. Level of aspiration. Theory				■	+.57	+.67	+.45	+.76	+.99	+.67	+.43	+.27	−.44	+.30	+.16	+.67	+.83	+.67	+.83	+.44	+.67	+.67	−.44
6. Level of aspiration. Method					■	+.44	+.67	+.76	+.15	+.93	−.30	+.80	+.80	+.89	+.73	+.84	+.15	+.15	+.67	+.15	−.67	+.15	−.15
7. Innovation						■	+.94	+.98	+.67	+.83	±0	+.93	+.93	+.89	+.95	+.84	+.67	+.44	+.67	+.44	+.15	+.15	−.15
8. Status outside the department							■	+.86	+.60	+.85	−.02	+.93	+.98	+.97	+.87	+.98	+.67	−.15	+.23	+.23	−.15	+.15	+.15
9. Status in peer-group								■	+.60	+.76	+.45	+.98	+.93	+.85	+.84	+.57	+.57	+.76	+.93	+.57	+.30	+.30	−.16
10. Status among students									■	+.76	+.76	+.91	+.30	+.99	+.17	+.83	+.83	+.83	+.83	+.83	+.44	+.15	−.30
11. Status among professors										■	+.67	+.30	+.80	+.30	+.17	+.84	−.15	−.15	+.44	+.44	+.15	−.15	+.66
12. Personal contact with professor											■	+.57	+.43	+.43	+.28	±0	+.30	−.15	−.30	−.30	−.30	−.68	±0
13. Marks in M.A., etc.												■	+.43	+.07	+.96	+.93	±0	±0	+.13	±0	−.30	+.32	−.19
14. Printed production													■	+1	+.97	+.93	+.30	+.30	+.30	+.30	−.30	+.30	−.30
16. Choice of career														■	+1	+.99	+.30	+.17	+.17	+.17	+.05	+.30	±0
18. Appointment at the department															+1	+1	+.17	+.17	+.48	+.44	+.48	+.18	+.17
20. Academic level of own teaching																■	+.67	+.67	+.83	+.44	+.15	+.16	−.15
21. Ability to teach																	■	+.44	+.67	+.67	+.83	+.15	−.15
23. Radicalism																		■	+.83	+.83	+.83	+.83	−.15
24. Level of aspiration for own teaching																			■	+.97	+.97	+.83	−.15
26. Production of teaching material																				■	+.83	+.67	+.44
27. Interest in teaching																					■	+.68	−.15
28. Interest in theoretical items																						■	+.15
29. Years at the department																							■

ability is, thus, a little reduced. Then it is likely that some variables might form clusters, each cluster with positive correlations between its variables, but negative correlations between variables from different clusters.

My own matrix, no. 2, delivers three clusters, one very large and two very small consisting only of teaching traits 26 (Production of teaching material) and 29 (Years in the department). Kerstin Bohm's matrix no. 3, gives a similar result as trait 29 forms a cluster of its own, but trait 26 in her estimations belongs to the large cluster.

We agree, however, that a large cluster completely dominates the matrix. There should be positive correlations between its traits. My own matrix has no more than 17 negative correlations out of 231 (7%) between the traits in this cluster, Kerstin Bohm's has 17 out of 253 (7%). Trait 29 should have negative correlations with the others. In my matrix it has only 7 positive correlations out of 23 (30%), in Kerstin Bohm's 8 (35%).

We disagree about trait 26, which also has a comparatively low reliability, +0.67. From my administrative point of view—which I think in this case gives a better perspective—Xerox and stencilled copies represent to the teachers an effort to compensate experience and research merits. Kerstin Bohm seems to consider them as a result of research training. Both of us think, however, that good teachers tend to produce more material and that years at the department do not increase the ability to teach.

The matrices give some insight in the teaching efforts at the department. They tend to be better the more qualified the teachers are. Higher posts as teachers tend to go to the most qualified, but years at the department do not seem to belong to these qualifications. Interest in teaching (27) seems to fall off among the independent (2) and the innovators (7), who probably are more interested in research. Interest in the theoretical items of the teaching (28) does not promote status among the professors or contacts with them (11, 12), nor the level of aspiration for own teaching.

When I try to test hypotheses deduced from the summation theory, the starting-point is the sign of the correlations. These signs then must be rather similar in our two matrices. We can compute a kind of matrix reliability by comparing the correlations of the traits Kerstin Bohm and I have estimated independent of one another (that is, variables 10, 21, 23, 24, 26 and 27). Zero correlations are, according to the summation theory, accepted as well as not negative within clusters as not positive between clusters. They are handled the same way in the following fourfold table:

Signs in matrix 3

$$\text{Signs in matrix 2} \quad \frac{+\ 82\ \mid\ 7}{-\ 17\ \mid\ 16} = +0.82$$

Most of the sign differences refer to variable 26, which we have placed in different clusters. Still, it does not decrease the correlation below +0.82.

I expected a moderate cluster formation among the 26 teachers as they have been selected so as to eliminate very poor teachers. If they had all of them been at the same level, I should, according to the summation theory, expect strong and clear-cut clusters. In order to reduce the dispersion of teaching ability, I divide the teachers into two groups: 13 good teachers and 13 less good. If I then compute the correlations between the traits within both of these two groups I expect that they will give clusters similar to matrix 2. There is a risk to use so small groups. Kerstin Bohm's data can be used as a kind of control, although her choice of 13 good teachers differs from mine.

My own matrix from the 13 good teachers is presented as matrix 4, page 86 and Kerstin Bohm's, page 87. What is the reliability between our signs of the correlation?

Signs in matrix 5

$$\text{Signs in matrix 4} \quad \frac{+\ 178\ \mid\ 17}{-\ 33\ \mid\ 25} = +0.78$$

This is a comparatively high correlation, since they are calculated from slightly different populations. And actually the two matrices give exactly the same clusters: one large and one small consisting of two variables: personal contact with the professor (12) and level of aspiration for own teaching (26). I interpret this as an indication that good teachers either have a good background in research and teaching or compensate these advantages with contacts and production of teaching material.

Both clusters are rather clear. The large cluster has 24 negative correlations out of 210 (11%) in matrix 4, 20 (10%) in matrix 5. The small cluster has 9 positive correlations out of 44 (20%) in matrix 4, but 43% in matrix 5.

What about the less good teachers? I expect, of course, them to give similar matrices whether I or Kerstin Bohm have estimated the teaching traits. My own matrix, nr 6, is presented in page 88, Kerstin Bohm's nr 7 in page 89. How similar are the signs of the corresponding correlations? They are presented in the following fourfold table:

Signs in matrix 7

		+	−	
Signs in matrix 6	+	172	26	= +0.82
	−	22	33	

The differences mainly refer to variable 26, which we have placed in different clusters, but the Q-coefficient still is as high as +0.82.

Both matrices have a large cluster of research variables, career variables and most of the teaching variables and a smaller cluster of the three teaching traits 23, 27 and 28, but my own matrix also presents, as I just hinted, this as an indication that less good teachers either have the traditional set of researchers' and teachers' traits or try to compensate them with radicalism (23), interest in teaching (27) and interest in the theoretical items in their teaching (28). My own matrix, no. 6, also indicates that according to my estimations production of stencilled or Xerox copies may be used as a substitute to both these clusters.

The large cluster is clear-cut, only 10 negative correlations out of 172 (6 %) in matrix 6, 20 negative out of 190 (11 %) in matrix 7. The smaller cluster (23, 27 and 28) is not so good: matrix 6 has 28 positive correlations out of 60 (47 %), matrix 7 has 20 positive out of 60 (33 %). Variable 26 has 6 positive correlations out of 22 (27 %) in matrix 6.

The summation theory has been applied to my material of 26 teachers at the department, to 13 good teachers and 13 less good. How did the theory turn out? Well, my own matrices generally gave clusters similar to Kerstin Bohm's and that is a kind of support to the theory.

Theoretically I also expect my own three matrices (2, 4 and 6) to present similar clusters. I can't say they do. The variables outside the large cluster have in the six presented matrices been:

	According to Bjurman	According to Bohm
Population of 26 teachers	26, 29	29
Population of 13 good teachers	12, 26	12, 26
Population of 13 less good teachers	26, 23, 27, 28	23, 27, 28

Variable 26 appears in 4 of 6 cases but otherwise there is no overlapping between the three populations. The summation theory presupposes,

Matrix 4. Correlations from a population of 13 good teachers, traits estimated by Bjurman

Variables	2	3	4	5	6	7	8	9	10	11	13	14	16	18	20	23	24	27	28	29	12	26
1. Ego strength	+1	+.74	+.05	+.93	−.43	+.05	+.20	+.64	+1	+.64	+.41	+.41	+.20	−.05	+.20	+.64	+.84	+.65	+.74	+.60	−.20	+.65
2. Independence, subject	■	+1	+.41	+1	+.71	+.41	+1	+.41	+1	+.92	+.91	+.71	+.83	+.71	+1	+.20	+.41	+.71	+.67	+.33	−.52	−.08
3. Independence, method		■	+1	+.74	+.74	+.28	+.74	+.74	+.33	+.74	+.71	+.86	+.67	+.85	+.14	+.74	+.58	+.74	+.74	+.84	−.67	+.33
4. Perseverance			■	+.74	+.74	+.93	+.94	+.20	−.14	+.64	+.41	+1	+.85	+1	+.74	+.64	−.41	+1	+.74	+.60	−.20	−1
5. Level of asp. Theory				■	+.05	+.74	+.74	+.64	+1	+.64	+.41	+1	+1	+1	+.74	+.64	+.84	+.14	+.14	+.66	−.74	+.66
6. Level of asp. Method[a]					■	+.20	+.74	+.64	−.50	+.74	+.41	+.40	+.20	+.04	+.74	+.87	+.58	+.20	+.74	+.43	−.74	+.33
7. Innovation						■	+1	+.64	−.14	+.74	+.11	+.11	+.67	+.43	+.67	+.20	+.33	+.65	+.14	+.60	−.67	−.14
8. Status outside department							■	+.67	+.20	+.14	+1	+1	+1	+1	+1	+.33	−.11	+.20	+.74	+.71	−.74	−.50
9. Status in peer-group								■	+.85	+.74	+1	+1	+.93	+1	+.62	+.20	+.33	+.14	+.33	−.05	−.67	−.14
10. Status among students									■	+.05	+1	−.08	+.79	+.60	+1	+.64	+.78	+.64	+.20	+.14	−.20	−.14
11. Status among professors										■	+.41	+.26	−.50	−.65	+.33	+1	−.33	−.14	+.71	−.41	−.11	−.70
13. Marks in M.A., etc.											■	+.41	−.74	+.60	+1	+.05	−.56	+.05	+.71	−.41	−.11	−.33
14. Printed production												■	+1	+1	+.20	+.41	−.56	+.41	+.67	+.05	−.20	−.33
16. Choice of career													■	+1	+1	+1	−.11	+.41	+.43	+.43	−.74	−.65
18. Appointment at department														■	+.94	+.85	−.33	+.74	+.67	−.20	−.43	−.50
20. Academic level of teaching															■	+.74	−.11	+.60	+.74	+.60	−.67	−.14
23. Radicalism																■	+.74	+.05	−.11	+.41	−.74	−.14
24. Level of asp. own teaching																	■	+.41	+1	+.60	−1	+1
27. Interest in teaching																		■	+1	+.41	−.20	+.66
28. Interest in theoretical items																			■	+.43	−.14	+.33
29. Years at the department																				■	−.43	+.14
12. Personal contact with professor																					■	+.14
26. Production teaching material																						■

Matrix 5. Correlations from a population of 13 good teachers, traits estimated by Kerstin Bohm

Variables	2	3	4	5	6	7	8	9	10	11	13	14	16	18	20	23	24	27	28	29	12	26
1. Ego strength	+.41	+.33	+.33	+.78	+.58	−.20	+.11	+.56	+.78	+.56	+.41	+.41	+.11	+.11	+.41	+.11	+.65	+.20	+.71	+.56	+.11	+.56
2. Independence, subject	■	+1	+.60	+1	−.43	+.41	+1	+.41	+.81	+.41	+.93	+.93	+.74	+.64	+.74	+.74	−.05	+.14	+.20	−.20	+.43	−.33
3. Independence, method		■	+.93	+.65	+.65	−.43	+1	+.41	+.65	+.83	+1	+1	+.05	+1	+.38	+.85	+.33	−.14	+.43	+.74	−.20	−.33
4. Perseverance			■	+.93	+.85	+.83	+.85	+.83	+.65	+.83	+1	+1	+1	+1	+.85	+.64	+.33	−.14	+.85	+.74	−.20	+.33
5. Level of asp. Theory				■	+.50	+1	+.50	+.78	+1	+.78	+1	+1	+.50	+.14	+1	+.65	+.65	+.33	+.50	+.33	−.11	−1
6. Level of asp. Method					■	+.50	+.14	+.71	+.78	+.71	+.20	+1	+.67	+.20	+.67	+.43	+.71	+.14	+.14	+.74	−.23	−1
7. Innovation						■	+.71	+.92	+.71	+.56	+1	+1	+1	+1	+.67	+.82	+.56	−1	+.71	+.58	−.58	−.20
8. Status outside department							■	+.71	+.78	+.71	+1	+1	+.94	+1	+.67	−.14	+.11	−1	+.14	+.45	−.46	+.11
9. Status in peer-group								■	+.11	−.20	+1	+1	+.71	+.41	+.71	+1	+.92	−.33	+.71	−.11	−.11	−1
10. Status among students									■	+.78	+1	+1	+.50	+.14	+1	+.65	+.78	+.33	+.51	+.33	−.33	−1
11. Status among professors										■	+.41	+1	+.71	+.41	+.11	−.41	−1	+.08	+.11	+1	+.11	−.20
13. Marks in M.A. etc.											■	+1	+1	+.93	+1	+.60	+.41	+.14	+.74	−.20	+.20	−.33
14. Printed production												■	+1	+.93	+1	+.60	+.41	+.14	+.74	−.20	+.20	−.33
16. Choice of career													■	+1	+.94	+.43	+.11	−.33	+.67	+.45	−.45	+.11
18. Appointment at department														■	+.20	+.60	−.33	+.14	+.74	+.43	−.43	−.82
20. Academic level of teaching															■	+.85	+.85	−.33	+.67	−.14	−.45	−.58
23. Radicalism																■	+.83	+.65	+.85	+.20	−.20	+.33
24. Level of asp. Own teaching																	■	+.78	+.11	+.11	−.58	+.56
27. Interest in teaching																		■	+1	+.33	+.50	+.78
28. Interest in theoretical items																			■	+.45	+.71	+.71
29. Years at the department																				■	−.14	+.65
12. Personal contact with professor																					■	+.11
26. Production of teaching material																						■

Matrix 6. Correlations from a population of 13 less good teachers, traits estimated by Bjurman

Variables	2	3	4	5	6	7	8	9	10	11	12	13	14	16	18	20	24*	29	26	23	27	28
1. Ego strength	+.43	+.64	+.83	+.93	+.93	+.93	+.93	+1	+.64	+.93	+.63	+.84	+.84	+.84	+.83	+1	−.41	+.63	−1	−.05	−.64	+.33
2. Independence, subject	■	+.85	+.71	−.20	+.85	+.85	+.94	+.94	+.85	+.85	+.38	+.94	+.94	+.94	+.71	+.67	+.11	+.90	−.20	−.74	−.85	−.67
3. Independence. method		■	+1	+.64	+1	+.93	+.94	+.85	+1	+.93	+.64	+1	+1	+1	+.91	+.85	+.33	−.05	+1	+.05	+.05	+.20
4. Perseverance			■	+.83	+1	+1	+1	+1	+1	+1	+.83	+1	+1	+1	+.92	+1	+.56	−.05	−1	+.05	+.33	+.20
5. Level of aspiration. Theory				■	+.74	+.64	+.81	+1	+1	+.64	+.05	+.43	+.43	+.43	+.33	+.84	−.41	+.41	−1	+.25	+.33	−.11
6. Level of aspiration. Method					■	+1	+1	+.85	+1	+1	+.74	+1	+1	+1	+1	+1	−.11	−.64	−.14	+.93	+.93	+.58
7. Innovation						■	+1	+1	+1	+.93	+.93	+1	+1	+1	+1	+.85	+.33	−.20	−.50	+.20	+.20	+.14
8. Status outside department							■	+.85	+1	+.93	+.74	+1	+1	+1	+.92	+1	−.41	+.60	−1	+.05	+.05	−.43
9. Status in peer-group								■	+1	+.93	+.64	+1	+1	+1	+.92	+.85	−.41	−.05	−1	+.05	+.43	+.20
10. Status among students									■	+1	+.65	+1	+1	+1	+1	+1	+.11	+.20	+.50	+.43	+.65	+.33
11. Status among professors										■	+1	+.93	+1	+1	+1	+1	+.08	+.14	−1	+.05	+.05	+.43
12. Personal contact professor											■	+.93	+1	+1	+.78	+1	+.33	−.05	−.15	−.60	−.60	−.83
13. Marks in M.A.. etc.												■	+.85	+.85	+.93	+1	+.11	+.20	−1	−.20	−.20	−.14
14. Printed production													■	+1	+1	+1	+.11	+.20	+.50	−.20	−.20	−.14
16. Choice of career														■	+1	+1	+.11	+.20	−1	−1	−1	−.14
18. Appointment at department															■	+1	+.92	+1	−1	−1	+1	−.11
20. Academic level of teaching																■	+.11	+1	−1	+.05	+.60	−.43
24. Level of asp. Own teaching																	■	+.41	+.08	+.33	+.33	−.71
29. Years at the department																		■	+.65	−1	−.41	−.20
26. Production of teaching material																			■	−.05	−.14	+.33
23. Radicalism																				■	+.93	+1
27. Interest in teaching																					■	+1
28. Interest in theoretical items																						■

Matrix 7. *Correlations from a population of 13 less good teachers, traits estimated by Kerstin Bohm*

Variables	2	3	4	5	6	7	8	9	10	11	12	13	14	16	18	20	24	26	29	23	27	28
1. Ego strength	+1	+.64	+.45	+.64	+1	+1	+1	+1	+.64	+1	+.27	+1	+1	+1	+1	+1	+.45	+.45	+1	+.27	−1	+.09
2. Independence. subject	■	+.64	+.33	−.14	+.85	+.83	+.83	+.64	−.14	+.83	+.05	+.93	+.93	+.93	+.83	+.83	+.33	+.33	+.74	−.60	−1	−.20
3. Independence. method		■	+.78	+.33	+1	+.78	+.78	+.65	+.33	+.78	+.14	+1	+1	+1	+.76	+1	+.78	+.78	+.33	+.33	−.14	+.50
4. Perseverance			■	+.02	+.78	+.92	+.56	+.83	+.78	+.92	+.83	+.83	+.83	+.83	+.92	+.92	+.56	+.56	−.11	+.33	+.08	−.58
5. Level of asp. Theory				■	+.71	+.08	+.08	+.65	+.90	+.08	−1	−.14	−.14	−.14	+.08	+.08	+.78	+.78	−.50	+1	+.33	+1
6. Level of asp. Method					■	+.50	+.08	+.84	−.33	+1	+.43	+1	+1	+1	+1	+.71	+.11	+.11	−.14	−.20	+1	+.14
7. Innovation						■	+1	+.92	+1	+.08	+.83	+1	+1	+1	+1	+1	+.56	+.56	+.58	−.41	−1	−.58
8. Status outside department							■	+.83	+.83	+.92	+.33	+1	+.93	+.93	+.92	+.92	−.20	−.20	−.11	−.41	−1	+1
9. Status in peer-group								■	+.65	+.08	+.08	+.64	+.93	+.93	+1	+1	+.83	+.83	+.20	+.05	−.14	+1
10. Status among students									■	+.65	−.14	−.14	−.14	+1	+.08	+.08	+.78	+.78	+.58	+1	+.90	+.50
11. Status among professors										■	+.08	+1	+1	+1	+1	+1	+.56	+.56	+.58	−.41	−1	−.58
12. Personal contact professor											■	+.83	+1	+1	+1	+.83	−.41	−.41	−.43	−.60	−.14	−1
13. Marks in M.A., etc.												■	+1	+1	+.83	+.83	+.33	+.33	+.20	−.60	−1	−.20
14. Printed production													■	+1	+1	+1	+.33	+.33	+.20	−.60	−1	−.20
16. Choice of career														■	+1	+1	+.33	+.33	+.20	−.60	−1	−.20
18. Appointment at department															■	+1	+.56	+.56	+.58	−.41	−1	−.58
20. Academic level of teaching																■	+.56	+.56	+.58	−.41	−1	−.58
24. Level of asp. Own teaching																	■	+1	+.58	+.83	+.78	+.71
26. Production of teaching material																		■	+.58	+.83	+.78	+.71
29. Years at the department																			■	−.43	−.50	−.14
23. Radicalism																				■	+1	+.85
27. Interest in teaching																					■	+.50
28. Interest in theoretical items																						■

however, that there should be similarities at least between the 13 good and the 13 less good teachers. If a variable is excluded from the large cluster in one of these populations because it has many negative correlations with the other variables, then it should at least tend to have many negative correlations in the other population too. I can test this hypothesis once I know the number of negative correlations that is to be defined as many. How many negative correlations do then the 23 variables have in the four populations of 13 teachers, two populations estimated by me and two by Kerstin Bohm. The distribution of 92 (4×23) is given below:

Number of negative correlations per variable	Number of variables
0	1
1	9
2	20
3	18
4	12
5	10
6	3
7	3
8	2
9	4
greater than 9	10

Evidently 6 and more negative correlations can be considered many. Then the similarities between the 23 variables in four matrices can be summarized in six fourfold tables:

		Matrix 5 Bohm 13 good teachers 1–5 neg. corr. / greater than 5	Matrix 6 Bjurman 13 less good teachers 1–5 neg. corr. / g. t. 5	Matrix 7 Bohm 13 less good teachers 1–5 neg. corr. / g. t. 5
Matrix 4 Bjurman 13 good teachers	1–5 neg. corr.	16 | 2	14 | 4	13 | 5
	g. t. 5 neg. corr.	3 | 2	3 | 2	3 | 2
Matrix 5 Bohm 13 good teachers	1–5 neg. corr.		16 | 3	15 | 4
	g. t. 5 neg. corr.		1 | 3	1 | 3
Matrix 6 Bjurman 13 less good teachers	1–5 neg. corr.			14 | 3
	g. t. 5 neg. corr.			2 | 4

These fourfold tables are used to compute Q-coefficients:

		Matrix 5 Bohm 13 good teachers	Matrix 6 Bjurman 13 less good teachers	Matrix 7 Bohm 13 less good teachers
Matrix 4 Bjurman	13 good teachers	+.68	+.40	+.27
Matrix 5 Bohm	13 good teachers		+.88	+.84
Matrix 6 Bjurman	13 less good teachers			+.81

The most important correlations of these six are those between matrices 4 and 6, that is matrices based on my estimations of good and of less good teachers and between matrices 5 and 7: Kerstin Bohm's estimations of good and less good teachers. These correlations are +0.40 and +0.84 with a mean at +0.62. This mean demonstrates that there is a tendency for variables with many negative correlations in one population of teachers to have many negative correlations also in the corresponding population. And that is what the summation theory leads us to expect.

Summing up my results, I am, as vice chairman of the department (studierektor), far more interested in the practical application of them than in the summation theory. From my point of view the most important results are the correlations between teaching ability and other factors among the 26 teachers with M.A., that is, how should teachers be selected among them. As it is, the Swedish law system says that appointments should be made according to merit and ability. This means in practice that applicants who have good marks, good publications and many years at the department as teachers (without misconduct) should be given priority. But among the teachers with M.A., teaching ability is, according to Kerstin Bohm's estimations, not correlated with marks in M.A. (± 0), publications in print (± 0) and years at the department (-15). My own estimations give negative correlations, with marks -0.32, with publications -0.43 and with years at the department -0.44. In my opinion we *have to* consider marks, publications and years at the department as important merits and we *should* do so in order to reward research but we also should pay attention to teaching ability, evaluated in some relevant way. Otherwise good teaching would not only lack reward, but even suffer.

Which factors seem to be associated with teaching ability? Ego-strength has the highest correlations, in my estimations +0.95, in Kerstin Bohm's +0.85, then status among students, in my matrix +0.84, in

Kerstin Bohm's +0.83. Ego strength and status among students have strong associations with one another, +0.93 in my matrix, +0.85 in Kerstin Bohm's. I interpret this as an indication that teaching at the department now is a rather frustrating experience. It is important to be able to withstand criticism, to admit "I don't know", "I will take a look in the literature and see if I can find an answer", etc. It is important not to lose contact with the students. If so, how can we reduce this frustration? One possibility is to give the teachers a free hand to handle their courses (but not the literature) in the way they want and to make the test their own way. In order to create contacts between teachers and students, teachers could take over one group of students and teach all their courses for half a year. The teachers would now hardly receive these suggestions well, as they have chosen the opposite way. In order to escape frustration, they try to reduce their contacts with the students and so they restrict their teaching to one or two courses and to short periods. In this way they build barriers between students and teachers.

Chapter 8

Research patterns among sociologists

Gunnar Boalt and Kerstin Bohm

Arne Bjurman has previously defined a number of traits used for the study of research behaviors (Chapter 7, pp. 73–92). They were chosen in order to test the idea that good researchers may differ in their sets of traits, as one set may compensate the lack of another, as predicted by the "summation theory", described for instance in Boalt–Lantz–Herlin: *The Academic Pattern*, chapter 3. Bjurman has studied a population of 67 sociologists, who had taken their M.A. examination at the University of Stockholm before 1973. He used 15 researchers' traits, 4 of them easily measured but 11 of them estimated by Bjurman and Boalt. The reliability was rather low, as the traits were to be estimated at the time when the subjects gained their M.A. (sometimes more than 20 years ago).

Bjurman has computed the correlations between the traits. If there were sets of traits able to substitute one another in research, we would expect the matrix of the correlations to split the variables in different clusters. But actually all traits tended to be positively correlated with one another, as only two out of 91 correlations were negative. This is, however, to be expected. If the population contains some very good researchers, some moderate and some bad; the good researchers tend to be good in many respects and the bad ones bad in many respects, which should result in positive correlations all over. But suppose that we took out the good researchers to form a group on their own. Then we might find clusters of traits positively correlated to the other traits within the cluster but negatively correlated to traits belonging to other clusters. Such a pattern would in our opinion indicate that good researchers tend to possess either the one cluster of traits or the other.

Technically it is possible that sets of traits have a high variation *within* different classes of researchers (very good, good, medium, moderate, and bad researchers) and a comparatively low variation *between* classes, and other sets a low variation within the classes of researchers but a high variance between them. If we use the printed scientific production to classify the researchers, we get five classes of them:

1. No scientific production, 8 M.A.s.
2. Some production but on a low level, 16 researchers.
3. 20 researchers who have written popular science, an article in a journal or a part of a book.
4. Scientific production at a high level but restricted in size, 16 researchers.
5. A large scientific production at a high level, 8 researchers.

Within each of these five groups we computed all correlations between our 15 researcher traits and brought them together in matrices in order to demonstrate the clusters—if any. Clusters formed by traits, positively correlated within the cluster but negatively correlated to traits in other clusters, indicate clusters competing with one another and so should tend to turn up in all five matrices. Only in the top class of researchers and the bottom class some deviance can be expected, as the top class may have chosen solutions not acceptable at lower levels, just as the bottom class may demonstrate different techniques of passing the M.A. examination without use of scientific ability.

The matrices do not contain variable 14, printed production, as it was used to separate the classes of researchers and we have changed the direction of variable 15, sex, so that it now is a scale of femininity.

Matrix 1, page 95, sums up the intercorrelations of the research traits among eight M.A.s with no printed production. There are two clusters: one large containing most of the traits, but ego strength (trait 1); personal contacts with professors (12) and female sex (15) form a second cluster. We interpret this pattern as an indication that most research traits accompany one another, but that they might be compensated by ego strength, help from the professors, female sex—and a tendency to leave the department (16) as they get neither appointment nor status there.

When we turn to matrix 2, page 95, with the correlations between the research traits among sixteen M.A.s with some production at a low scientific level, we expect to find clusters similar to those in matrix 1. Actually three of the four variables deviating from the research cluster in matrix 1, do deviate also in matrix 2.

Matrix 1 of correlations between 14 traits. 8 researchers with no production

Variables	1	12	15	7	8	2	9	11	3	4	5	6	13	16
1. Ego strength	■													
12. Personal contact with professors	±0	■												
15. Sex: 1 man, 2 women	+.8	+.8	■											
7. Innovation	+0	+.8	−.8	■										
8. Status outside the department	−.8	+.8	+.8	±0	■									
2. Independence in choice of subject	−.8	+0	−.8	+.8	+.8	■								
9. Status in peer group	±0	±0	+0	+.8	+.8	+1	■							
11. Status among professors	+0	+0	+.8	+.8	+.8	+.8	+.8	■						
3. Independence in method	−.8	−.8	−.8	−1	±0	+0	+.8	+.8	■					
4. Perseverance	−.8	−.8	−.8	−1	+0	+.8	+.8	+.8	+.8	■				
5. Level of aspiration. Theory	−.8	−.8	−1	+.8	±0	+.8	+.8	+.8	+.8	−1	■			
6. Level of aspiration. Method	−.8	−.8	−1	±0	+0	+.8	+.8	+.8	+.8	+1	+1	■		
13. Marks in M.A., etc.	±0	±0	−.8	+.8	+.8	+1	+1	+.8	+.8	+.8	+.8	+.8	■	
16. Withdrawal from the department	+1	±0	+1	−1	−1	−1	−1	−1	−1	−1	−1	−1	−1	■

Matrix 2 of correlations between 14 traits. 16 researchers with some production, but at a low level

Variables	2	15	3	4	5	6	7	8	9	11	12	13	16
2. Independence in choice of subject	■												
15. Sex: 1 man, 2 women	−.25	■											
1. Ego strength	+.47	±0											
3. Independence in method	+.47	−.25	■										
4. Perseverance	−.91	−.91	+1	■									
5. Level of aspiration. Theory		−.25	+.96	+.96	■								
6. Level of aspiration. Method		−.25	+.96	+.96	+.96	■							
7. Innovation	−.47	−.25	+.47	+.47	+.80	+.80	■						
8. Status outside the department	+.47	−1	+0	+0	+.47	+.47	+0	■					
9. Status in the peer group	−.47	−.25	+.47	+.47	+.80	+.80	+.47	+.47	■				
11. Status among professors	+.96	−.25	+.96	+.80	+.96	+.80	+.80	+.47	+.96	■			
12. Personal contact with professors	−.47	−.91	+.80	+.80	+.47	+.80	+.80	+.47	+.80	+.80	■		
13. Marks in M.A., etc.	−.50	±0	+0	+0	−.50	+.50	+.50	±0	+.50	+.50	+1	■	
16. Withdrawal from the department	+.25	+.91	−.25	−.25	−.25	−.25	−.25	−.25	−.25	−.67	−.15	−.91	■

95

Trait 1, ego strength, has, however, this time joined the large research cluster, but in matrix 3, page 97, it has withdrawn from the large research cluster again and forms a little cluster of its own. Matrix 4, page 97, shows the two usual clusters, although trait 15, sex has a negative correlation with trait 2, independence in choice of subject for the M.A. thesis. Matrix 5, page 98 lacks the variables 15, sex, and 16, withdrawal, as all eight of our top researchers are men and full professors. Trait 2, independence in choice of subject this time has joined the large research cluster. The small, deviating cluster this time consists of variables 1, 5 and 7, indicating that good researchers either possess the usual set of research traits or have enough ego strength, ability for theory and innovation to dispense with status and perfectionistic traits. But evidently the sex trait (15) and the withdrawal trait (16) have been influential in the selection of this top group, as no women and no withdrawals are left in it.

We expected in advance that some research traits should have far more variance between the classes of researchers than within them and so tend to be excluded from the rest, not belonging to the clusters. The two extreme groups may, however, deviate a little from the rest, as there might be particular solutions open to very good researchers or to the bottom class, just able to pass the M.A. examination. We test these hypotheses in the following table:

Trait number	Traits not belonging to the large research cluster in matrix no.				
	1	2	3	4	5
1. Ego strength	×	−	×	×	×
2. Independence in choice of subject	−	×	×	×	−
15. Sex (Femininity)	×	×	×	×	[a]
16. Withdrawal from the department	×	×	×	×	[b]
5. Level of aspiration. Theory	−	−	−	−	×
7. Innovation	−	−	−	−	×
11. Status among professors	×	−	−	−	−

[a] No femininity, as the whole sample consists of men.
[b] No withdrawal, as the whole sample consists of full professors.

The table demonstrates that the traits 1, 2, 15 and 16 in most cases do not belong to the large research cluster and that the two extreme samples are

Matrix 3 of correlations between 14 traits, 20 researchers who have written popular science, articles in journals or a part of a book

Variables	1	2	15	3	4	5	6	7	8	9	11	12	13	16
1. Ego strength	■													
2. Independence in choice of subject	−.38	■												
15. Sex: 1 man. 2 women	−.1	+.39	■											
3. Independence in method	−.38	−.38	+.39	■										
4. Perseverance	+.72	−.88	−.39	+.72	■									
5. Level of aspiration. Theory	±0	−.38	+.39	+.72	+.72	■								
6. Level of aspiration. Method	+.38	−.88	−.39	+.72	+.88	+.72	■							
7. Innovation	±0	−.38	+.39	+.72	+.88	+.72	+.72	■						
8. Status outside the department	+.38	+.38	−.39	+.38	+.38	−.38	±0	+.38	■					
9. Status in the peer group	−.38	−.38	+.39	+.72	+.72	+.72	+.38	+.38	+.88	■				
11. Status among professors	+.38	−.38	+.39	+.38	+.72	+.38	+.38	+.38	+.99	±0	■			
12. Personal contact with professors	+.38	−.72	+.39	+.72	+.88	+.38	+.72	+.38	+.99	+.88	+.72	■		
13. Marks in M.A.. etc.	−.38	−.38	+.39	+.72	+.38	±0	+.72	+.72	+.38	+.72	+.38	+.99	■	
16. Withdrawal from the department	−.20	+.56	+.50	−.56	−.80	−.56	−.56	−.56	−.56	−.80	−.80	−.56	−.56	■

Matrix 4 of correlations between 14 traits, 16 researchers with a restricted scientific production of a high level

Variables	1	2	15	3	4	5	6	7	8	9	11	12	13	16
1. Ego strength	■													
2. Independence in choice of subject	+.8	■												
15. Sex: 1 man. 2 women	±0	−1	■											
3. Independence in method	±0	−.47	−1	■										
4. Perseverance	+.8	+.8	−1	±0	■									
5. Level of aspiration. Theory	+.47	+.47	−1	+.47	+.96	■								
6. Level of aspiration. Method	±0	−.47	±0	+.47	±0	±0	■							
7. Innovation	±0	−.47	−1	+.8	+.47	+.47	+.47	■						
8. Status outside the department	+.47	±0	±0	±0	±0	±0	+.8	±0	■					
9. Status in the peer group	±0	−.47	−1	+.47	+.47	+.80	+.47	+.47	+.8	■				
11. Status among professors	+.47	±0	−1	+.47	+.47	+.80	+.8	+.8	+.47	+.96	■			
12. Personal contact with professors	±0	±0	−1	+.8	+.47	+.80	+.47	+.8	±0	+.8	+.96	■		
13. Marks in M.A.. etc.	±0	+.47	−1	±0	+.47	+.80	+.8	+.47	±0	+.8	+.47	+.96	■	
16. Withdrawal from the department	±0	+.50	+1	−.50	−.50	−.84	−.50	−.84	−.84	−.50	−.84	−.50	−.50	■

Matrix 5 of correlations between 12 variables, 8 researchers with a large scientific production at a high level

Variables	1	5	7	2	3	4	6	8	9	11	12	13	15
1. Ego strength	■	+.8	+.8	±0	±0	+.8	-.8	±0	+.8	±0	-.8	+.8	
5. Level of aspiration. Theory		■	+.8	±0	-.8	-.8	±0	-.8	±0	-.8	-1	±0	
7. Innovation			■	+.8	±0	±0	±0	±0	+.8	±0	-.8	±0	
2. Independence in choice of subject				■	+.8	+.8	+1	±0	+.8	+.8	±0	±0	
3. Independence in method					■	+.8	+.8	+.8	+.8	+1	+.8	+.8	
4. Perseverance						■	+.8	+.8	+.8	+1	+.8	+.8	
6. Level of aspiration. Method							■	±0	±0	+.8	±0	±0	
8. Status outside the department								■	±0	+.8	+.8	+.8	
9. Status in the peer group									■	+.8	+.8	+.8	
11. Status among professors										■	+.8	+.8	
12. Personal contact with professors											■	±0	
13. Marks in M.A., etc.												■	
15. Sex: 1 man. 2 women													■

Neither variable 15, sex, nor variable 16, withdrawal from the department, can be applied to this sample, as all of these eight researchers are men and have chairs at sociological departments.

the only ones where the traits 5, 7 and 11 have been excluded from it. Our hypotheses, thus, cannot be confuted.

What does this say about the selection and career of the researchers? Evidently that in order to advance from a lower to a higher class of researchers it is important not to be a woman (trait 15), not to withdraw from the sociological departments (trait 16), not to have ego strength (trait 1) and not to choose subject for the thesis independently (trait 2). But all the other traits do promote promotion, especially the traits Independence in method (3), Perseverance (4), Level of aspiration for methods (6) and Status in peer group (9), which traits generally are highly correlated with one another and with most other traits in the large research cluster.

This is an important conclusion and easy to interpret. The academic community is a male community. Women are at a decided disadvantage. Scientific work of high class must be done in contact with those who set the example and evaluate the result. Ego strength is dangerous, as ego-strong researchers often pursue their own objects, paying too little attention to professors and previous research. Independence in choice of subject for the M.A. thesis generally means that the candidate is a civil servant or employed by a company to investigate a special problem independently of the professor's wishes. This might give him a M.A. degree but seldom anything more. And then at last the traits most important to the academic ideal of perfectionism promote the scientific production and career.

Bjurman and Boalt tried to estimate the research traits at the time the researchers passed their M.A. examination. We risk, of course, a halo effect, giving too high marks to the researchers, who later made a good career. This halo effect would, however, make us overrate for instance the eight researchers with a large production at a high level in a similar way and so influence the correlations in matrix 5, page 98, rather little. The same discussion applies, of course, to the matrices 1–4, and so we believe we may disregard the halo effect.

We have, thus, successfully tested one part of the summation theory and now turn to another. If a sample of researchers varies very much in research ability, it will be dominated by the good researchers possessing research traits to a high degree and by bad researchers lacking them. This creates positive correlations between the research traits. But if we exclude the best and the worst researchers in our sample, this will reduce the variation between classes of researchers for some variables, which might result in some negative correlations. The more homogeneous our sample of researchers is made, the more strongly negative correlations will the matrix contain.

We test this hypothesis with four different samples selected among our 67 researchers, no sample above 34 or below 16, as the size of the sample does influence the size of the correlations to some degree. Our four samples were:

1. 34 researchers, 17 of them with the best production, 17 of them with the worst. This sample evidently has a strong variation between classes.
2. 34 researchers with at least good scientific production. Variation between classes then is reduced.
3. 20 researchers of medium capacity, the best and the worst excluded. Variation between classes somewhat reduced, but still not negligible as these researchers might have written popular science, articles in journals or a part of a book.
4. 16 researchers with a restricted scientific production at a high level. This sample is the most homogeneous and variation between classes should be low.

We expect that the correlations between the research traits should have strong positive correlations and few or no negative correlations in our first sample. When we make the samples more homogeneous, strong positive correlations decrease and strong negative correlations increase, until we get bimodal distributions.

This hypothesis is tested on the four distribution curves, page 101, showing the distribution of the correlations. Sample 1 has, as we expected, few and weak negative correlations, many and strong positive correlations. Sample 2 has more negative correlations and the positive ones are weakened. Sample 4 is a good case of a bimodal curve and sample 3 comes in, as it should, between 2 and 4. Our hypothesis then is not refuted.

We now leave the summation hypothesis for a while and turn to some aspects on researchers. Which researchers remain at the department? How are they able to do so? Thirty-four of our sixty-seven did remain at some kind of sociological department. We expect, of course, that M.A.s with high marks tend to stay.

	Withdrawn	Remaining	% remaining
M.A. with 2 points	5	3	38
M.A. with 2½ points	14	10	42
M.A. with 3 points	14	23	62

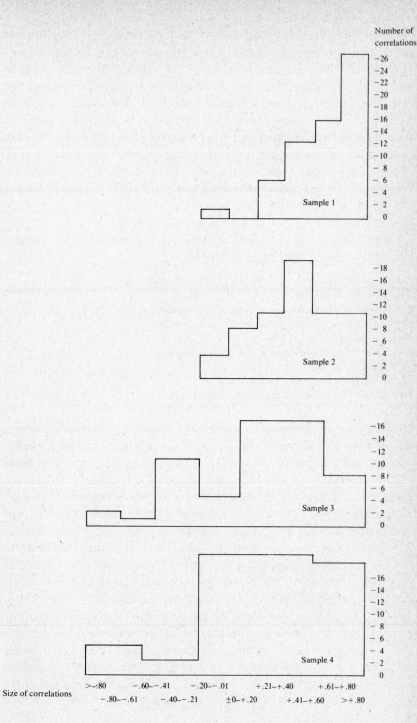

Evidently the tendency to withdraw is much higher among those who had got low marks. But we already know that withdrawal as well as ego strength and independence in choice of subject tend to hinder research and career, to be negatively correlated with the research traits within the five classes of researchers, while the perfectionistic research traits, such as 3, 4, 6 and 9, are rewarded. The researchers lacking these traits not only tend to be eliminated and to give up research, they also develop symptoms of alienation. Such symptoms are difficult to measure, but low status at the department, trouble with alcohol and divorce could be considered. To test this idea we made a scale of perfectionism by adding the given points for the four traits 3 (Independence in method), 4 (Perseverance), 6 (Level of aspiration, Method) and 9 (Status in peer group) to a sum. These Perfectionism scales give the following correlations with different indicators of alienation:

Correlation between Perfectionism (3+4+6+9) and Withdrawal from the department	−0.65
Correlation between Perfectionism and giving up research	−0.85
Correlation between Perfectionism and no room of one's own at the department	−0.70
Correlation between Perfectionism and alcohol trouble (2 cases)	−1
Correlation between Perfectionism and divorce	+0.02
Correlation between Perfectionism and female sex	−0.63

Divorce gave no correlation but our other indications did. Perfectionists do not need to withdraw or to give up research, nor have they trouble with alcohol, but they do get rooms of their own and they tend to be men.

Perfectionism is evidently an advantage to researchers, but does it make them happier? It represents after all a heavy burden, makes research the only acceptable form of life. A perfectionist might accept administrative work at the department or university level for a while, as it has to be done, gives some status—and leaves some time for research. But teaching has little appeal to perfectionists. Teaching means cooperation with others, takes much time and demands contacts with students, generally uninterested in or critical of the perfectionistic rules of research. The students' questions are not only difficult to answer but their critique may also influence the teacher, make him more sceptical towards traditional ideals. Perfectionistic researchers should then prefer research or even administration to teaching. This tendency is not so pronounced among professors, who have a small teaching load and are to do research anyhow. But even junior researchers have to live and if they cannot get grants, they must go to administration or—driven to the utmost—teach. In order to demonstrate how perfectionists and imperfectionists choose, we classify the 28 researchers with M.A. from Stockholm University and employed at the universities in Stockholm, Linköping and Örebro according to their academic rank and their type of work in 1972. The perfectionists had more than 13 points from the traits 3, 4, 6 and 9, the imperfectionists less than 14 points.

	Perfectionists in			Imperfectionists in		
	Re-search	Admin.	Teach-ing	Re-search	Admin.	Teach-ing
3 Full professors and 1 associate professor	2	1	1	–	–	–
Lecturers with tenure (ord. universitetslektorer)	5	–	–	–	–	2
Other M.A.s employed at the departments	2	2	4	–	1	7

The perfectionists tend to avoid teaching, the imperfectionists to prefer it. As professors and lecturers with tenure are academically better qualified, they have less difficulty in obtaining grants and can go in for research, but if we compare only the least qualified M.A.s, they still show the same tendency.

We interpret the table as an indication that imperfectionists have a more positive attitude to teaching and students than the perfectionists. Probably they need the contacts and the status students can give them, in order to compensate their lack of perfectionism. If so they also need their peer groups better for the same reason. Can we test this hypothesis? Yes, it is easy to point out some of the groups, such as luncheon groups and leisure groups.

There were two large luncheon groups. One of them (8 members) brought food with them and took their luncheon together in a room at the ninth floor. Another group (8 members) went to the university restaurant and took their luncheon there. The ninth floor had a group throwing darts (5 members) and another played ping-pong (5 members). The eighth floor had a squash group (5 members). Four men used to play chess.

We computed for each of the 26 M.A.s at the department, 14 perfectionists and 12 imperfectionists; how many groups they belonged to:

	Number of group memberships			
	0	1	2	3
Perfectionists	5	4	4	1
Imperfectionists	2	4	3	3

Imperfectionists seem to belong to more groups and we believe that they do so in order to compensate their lack of perfectionism. When we suggested this to the perfectionists in our own research group, they protested vigorously. They pointed out first that they themselves felt their perfectionism as a very heavy burden and then that full professors at the university tended to form rather important groups with their colleagues at other departments and so should either be excluded from the comparisons or be given some extra memberships.

It is easy to exclude the three full professors and it is quite possible that more perfectionistic perfectionists need group memberships better than less perfectionistic perfectionists. We test this idea in a table:

	Number of group memberships			
	0	1	2	3
Perfectionists above 15 points	–	2	2	1
Perfectionists, 14–15 points	2	2	2	–

Evidently more perfectionistic perfectionists seem to need their groups more than the less perfectionistic perfectionists. But then the same tendency should hold also among the imperfectionists:

	Number of group memberships			
	0	1	2	3
Imperfectionists, 12–13 points	–	–	3	3
Imperfectionists below 12 points	2	4	–	–

More perfectionistic imperfectionists actually do belong to more groups than less perfectionistic imperfectionists. In this way we have got a splendid example of variation between and within classes. We believe, however, that the important thing actually is the low status of imperfectionists below 12 points. They probably badly need contacts and status in the groups but the members in these groups will not accept them and so they are isolated from peer groups.

Chapter 9

The selection of full professors in sociology

Ulla Bergryd

Bjurman and Bohm have, in the previous chapters, discussed the selection and grading of teachers and researchers. The full professors have, however, not been discussed although they supervise the researchers, grade their theses and influence the allocation of grants. How are the professors themselves then selected and appointed? In Sweden this is a complicated procedure, regulated by the university statute. When the scope of the chair has been defined, the president of the university announces it as vacant. Those who consider themselves competent apply for the chair, enumerating their merits and sending in their publications. The faculty then selects three full professors, generally two from Sweden and one from some other Scandinavian country to evaluate the merits and publications of the candidates and to rank them. These experts work independently of one another, but towards the end of their work the candidates are invited to give trial lectures in order to demonstrate their teaching ability to the experts and the faculty. The experts then are expected to discuss the candidates before they present their reports to the faculty. If the three experts unanimously pronounce themselves in favor of a candidate, the faculty always endorses their selection but the outcome is less predictable if the experts do not agree. On the basis of the experts' reports the faculty draws up a nomination list, and also declares which of the candidates are qualified for the chair. The faculty's proposal and the reports of the experts are sent to the Chancellor of the Universities and then to the ministry of education. The government makes the appointment.

The experts' reports evaluate the scientific ability of the candidates and the merits of their publications. The reports are so detailed and careful that it is possible to apply content analysis to them. Sometimes a candidate is so superior to the others that the experts can be given the simpler task to decide this question. These reports are short and hardly possible to use for my purpose. My material then consists of six cases, where chairs in sociology have been filled: Stockholm in 1954, Lund in 1955, Gothenburg in 1960, Uppsala in 1968, Lund in 1970 and Stockholm in 1972. Each case but the last has used three sociologists as experts, but at Stockholm in 1972 one expert was an economist. These cases give me a total of 71 reports by 9 different experts about 16 different candidates. The reports cannot be said to be independent of one another, as the experts always have discussed the candidates and in some cases have to evaluate candidates, which they have evaluated previously. The last point may be a bit inconvenient but has happened only in 13 cases. The interaction between the experts is, however, not to be ignored, and should, on the contrary, be considered in some of the hypotheses.

I have used 22 categories to cover the most relevant aspects of the reports and of the background of the candidates. They were a priori brought together in five groups:

I. *Basic scientific categories*
1. Number of excellent publications, characterized as "Very good work", "At a high level", etc.
2. Number of innovations in theory, method or application.
3. Publications with good, preferably new, theory. 1. No 2. Yes
4. Publications with good, preferably new, method. 1. No 2. Yes
5. Number of publications designated as useful to society.
6. The candidates research trend: 1. Not rising 2. Rising

II. *Additional scientific categories*
7. Number of publication titles cited by the expert in his report.
8. Number of research publication titles cited by the expert in his report.
9. Number of printed text books (>100 pp.) cited by the expert in his report.
10. Number of printed books (>100 pp.), including text books, cited by the expert.
11. The candidate has worked in the same research field as the expert. 1. No 2. Yes
12. The candidate possibly can reciprocate the appreciation of the expert. 1. No 2. Yes

III. *The trial lectures*

13. The trial lecture made 1. no impression 2. a good impression

IV. *Categories influenced by administrative factors*

14. The candidate supposed to "suit" the faculty. 1. No 2. Yes
15. The candidate's ability to cover the scope of the chair. 1. Not very good 2. Very good
16. The production of the candidate. 1. Partly outside 2. Wholly inside the scope of the chair.

V. *Categories covering relations with experts, competence, rank on nomination list and year of the case*

17. The candidate belongs to the same department as the expert 1. No 2. Yes
18. The candidate belongs to the same faculty as the expert 1. No 2. Yes
19. The candidate is declared competent by the expert. 1. No 2. Yes
20. Rank on the nomination list of the expert. 1. Low 2. High
21. Rank on the nomination list of the faculty. 1. Low 2. High
22. Year of the case. 1. Before 1967 2. After 1967

These 22 variables have first been counted (categories 1, 2, 7, 8, 9 and 10) or estimated on 5 point scales, then dichotomized with convenient lines near the median, which varies in my different samples. Then all the intercorrelations between the categories may be computed with Yule's Q-coefficient. The raw data are given in the table page 109.

This type of content analysis has drawbacks as an expert often avoids to use a category for reasons not possible to ascertain. He might consider the category too sacred for use in practice or too empty. Which tendency will dominate? Does a high frequency of grade 2 in my first eleven categories indicate that the expert who has used many 2:s of a particular category has high or little regard for it? In order to decide this point, I have to make a simple validity test, correlating the number of 2:s and the reliability coefficient of each category with its effect on (correlation with) high place in the nomination lists of the experts and of the faculties. The content analysis categories then give the following correlations:

Number of 2:s correlated with correlation category-nomination by experts	−0.5
Number of 2:s correlated with correlation category-nomination by faculty	−0.4
Reliability coefficient correlated with correlation category-nomination by experts	−0.8
Reliability coefficient correlated with correlation category-nomination by faculties	−0.4

Table on evaluations of content analysis categories from the experts' reports according to case, expert, place of the candidates on the nomination list and categories

Case	Expert	Candidate	1	2	3	4	5	6	7	8	9	10	11	12	13	14	15	16	19	20	21
Sthlm 54	Segerstedt	Boalt	2	1	1	1	2	2	2	1	2	2	2	2	1	2	2	2	2	1	1
		Carlsson	2	1	1	1	2	2	2	2	2	2	2	2	1	2	2	2	2	2	2
		Karlsson	2	1	2	1	1	2	2	2	2	2	2	2	1	1	2	2	2	3	3
		Dahlström	1	1	1	1	1	1	1	2	1	2	2	2	1	2	2	2	2	4	5
		Munch	2	1	2	1	1	1	2	1	1	1	1	2	1	1	1	1	2	5	4
		Hanssen	1	1	1	1	1	1	1	1	1	1	1	1	1	1	2	1	1	6	6
		Malmsten	1	1	1	1	1	1·	1	1	1	1	1	1	1	1	2	1	1	7	7
		Number of 2:s	4	0	2	0	2	3	4	3	3	4	4	5	0	3	6	4	5		
	Wikman	Carlsson	2	1	1	1	1	1	2	2	2	2	1	1	2	2	2	2	2	1	2
		Munch	2	1	1	1	1	1	2	2	1	1	2	2	1	1	2	1	2	2	4
		Boalt	2	1	1	1	1	1	1	1	2	2	1	2	2	1	1	1	1		
		Hanssen	2	2	1	2	1	2	2	2	1	1	2	2	2	2	2	2	2	4	6
		Karlsson	2	1	1	1	1	2	1	1	2	2	1	2	1	1	1	2	2	5	3
		Dahlström	1	1	1	1	1	1	1	1	1	2	1	1	1	2	1	1	1	6	5
		Malmsten	1	1	1	1	1	2	2	1	1	1	1	2	1	1	1	1	1	7	7
		Number of 2:s	5	1	0	1	0	3	4	3	3	4	2	4	3	4	2	6	4		
	Husén	Boalt	2	2	1	2	1	2	1	2	2	2	2	2	2	2	2	2	2	1	1
		Carlsson	2	2	1	2	1	2	2	1	2	2	2	2	2	2	2	2	2	2	2
		Karlsson	2	1	1	1	1	2	1	2	2	2	1	2	1	1	2	2	2	3	3
		Dahlström	1	1	1	1	1	2	1	2	1	2	1	1	1	2	2	2	2	4	5
		Munch	1	1	1	1	1	1	2	1	1	1	1	1	1	1	2	1	2	5	4
		Hanssen	1	1	1	1	1	1	2	1	1	1	1	1	1	2	2	1	1	6	6
		Malmsten	1	1	1	1	1	1	2	1	1	1	1	1	1	1	2	1	1	7	7
		Number of 2:s	3	2	0	2	0	4	4	3	3	4	2	3	2	3	7	4	5		
Lund 55	Boalt	Carlsson	2	2	2	2	2	1	2	2	2	2	2	2	2	2	2	2	2	1	1
		Karlsson	1	1	1	1	1	2	1	1	2	2	2	2	1	1	2	2	2	2	3
		Pfannenstill	1	1	1	1	1	2	2	1	1	2	2	2	2	2	1	1	3	2	
		Hanssen	1	1	1	1	1	1	2	2	1	1	1	1	1	1	2	1	4	4	
		Number of 2:s	1	1	1	1	1	2	3	2	2	3	3	3	2	2	3	3	2		
	Segerstedt	Carlsson	2	1	1	1	2	2	2	2	2	2	2	2	2	2	2	2	2	1	1
		Karlsson	2	1	2	1	1	2	1	1	2	1	2	2	1	2	2	2	2	2	3
		Pfannenstill	1	1	1	1	1	2	2	1	1	2	2	1	1	1	1	1	3	2	
		Hanssen	1	1	1	1	1	1	1	2	1	1	1	1	1	1	1	1	4	4	
		Number of 2:s	2	0	1	0	1	2	2	3	2	1	3	3	1	2	2	2	2		
	Wikman	Pfannenstill	1	1	1	1	1	2	2	1	1	2	1	2	2	2	2	2	2	1	2
		Carlsson	2	1	1	1	1	1	2	2	2	2	1	1	2	2	1	2	2	2	1
		Hanssen	1	2	1	2	2	2	2	1	2	2	1	1	1	2	2	2	3	4	
		Karlsson	1	1	1	1	1	2	1	1	2	2	1	1	1	2	2	2	4	3	
		Number of 2:s	1	1	0	1	0	3	3	2	2	3	1	2	2	3	4	4			
Göteborg 60	Boalt	Dahlström	2	2	1	2	2	1	2	2	2	2	2	2	2	2	2	2	1	1	
		Karlsson	1	1	1	1	1	1	1	1	2	1	2	2	2	1	2	2	2	2	2
		Number of 2:s	1	1	0	1	1	0	1	1	2	1	2	2	2	1	2	2	2	1	1
	Segerstedt	Karlsson	2	1	1	1	1	1	1	1	2	1	2	2	1	1	2	2	2	1	2
		Dahlström	1	1	1	1	1	1	2	2	2	2	2	2	1	2	2	2	2	2	1
		Number of 2:s	1	0	0	0	0	0	1	1	2	1	2	2	0	1	2	2	2	1	1

Case	Expert	Candidate		Categories																		
			1	2	3	4	5	6	7	8	9	10	11	12	13	14	15	16	19	20	21
	Carlsson	Dahlström	1	1	1	1	2	1	1	1	2	2	2	2	2	2	2	2	2	1	1
		Karlsson	1	1	1	1	1	1	2	2	2	1	2	2	2	1	2	2	2	2	2
		Number of 2:s	0	0	0	0	1	0	1	1	2	1	2	2	2	1	2	2	2	1	1
Uppsala 68	Allardt	Israel	2	2	2	2	2	1	2	2	2	2	2	2	1	1	2	2	2	1	2
		Himmelstrand	2	1	2	2	1	2	2	2	1	1	1	2	1	2	2	2	2	2	1
		Lindskog	1	1	1	1	1	1	1	1	1	1	1	2	1	2	1	2	1	3	3
		Bjerstedt	1	2	1	2	1	1	1	1	2	2	1	1	1	1	1	2	1	4	4
		Number of 2:s	2	2	2	3	1	1	2	2	2	2	1	3	0	2	2	4	2		
	Boalt	Himmelstrand	2	1	1	1	1	1	1	1	1	1	1	2	2	2	2	2	2	1	1
		Israel	2	2	1	1	2	1	2	2	2	2	1	2	1	1	2	2	2	2	2
		Lindskog	1	1	1	1	1	1	1	1	1	1	1	1	2	2	1	2	1	3	3
		Bjerstedt	2	1	1	1	1	1	2	2	2	2	1	2	1	1	1	1	1	4	4
		Number of 2:s	3	1	0	0	1	0	2	2	2	2	0	3	2	2	2	3	2		
	Dahlström	Israel	1	2	2	1	1	2	2	2	2	2	2	2	2	2	2	2	2	1	2
		Himmelstrand	2	2	1	2	1	2	2	2	1	1	2	2	1	1	2	2	2	2	1
		Lindskog	1	1	1	1	1	1	1	1	1	1	1	1	1	1	1	1	1	3	3
		Bjerstedt	2	1	1	1	1	1	1	1	1	2	1	1	1	1	1	1	1	4	4
		Number of 2:s	2	2	2	0	1	0	2	2	1	2	2	2	1	1	2	2	2		
Lund 70	Allardt	Israel	2	2	2	2	2	1	2	2	2	2	2	2	1	2	2	2	2	1	1
		Swedner	2	1	1	1	2	1	2	2	2	2	2	2	1	1	2	2	2	2	3
		Korpi	2	2	2	2	1	2	1	1	1	1	2	2	1	2	1	2	2	3	2
		Lindskog	1	1	1	1	1	1	1	1	1	1	1	2	1	1	1	1	1	4	4
		Number of 2:s	3	2	2	2	2	1	2	2	2	2	3	4	0	2	2	3	3		
	Dahlström	Israel	2	2	2	1	1	1	2	2	2	2	2	2	1	2	2	2	2	1	1
		Korpi	2	2	1	2	1	2	1	1	1	1	2	2	1	2	2	2	2	2	2
		Swedner	1	1	1	1	2	1	2	2	2	2	1	2	1	1	2	2	2	3	3
		Lindskog	1	1	1	1	1	1	1	1	1	1	1	1	1	1	1	1	1	4	4
		Number of 2:s	2	1	2	0	1	1	2	2	2	2	2	3	0	2	3	3	3		
	Lysgaard	Israel	2	2	1	1	1	1	2	2	2	2	2	2	1	2	2	2	2	1	1
		Swedner	1	1	2	2	1	1	2	2	2	2	2	2	1	1	2	2	2	2	3
		Korpi	2	1	1	1	1	2	1	1	1	1	2	1	1	2	2	2	2	3	2
		Lindskog	1	1	1	1	1	1	1	1	1	1	1	2	1	1	1	1	1	4	4
		Number of 2:s	2	1	1	1	0	1	2	2	2	2	3	3	0	2	3	3	3		
Sthlm 72	Boalt	Korpi	2	2	2	1	1	1	1	2	2	1	2	2	1	2	2	2	2	1	1
		Swedner	1	1	1	1	1	2	2	2	2	2	2	1	1	1	2	2	2	2	2
		Rundblad	1	1	1	1	1	2	2	1	1	1	2	2	1	2	1	2	1	3	3
		Börjesson	1	1	1	2	1	2	1	1	2	2	2	1	1	1	1	2	1	4	4
		Number of 2:s	1	1	1	1	0	3	2	2	3	2	4	2	0	2	2	4	2		
	Sveri	Swedner	1	1	1	1	1	1	1	2	1	1	1	1	1	1	2	2	2	1	2
		Korpi	1	2	1	1	1	2	2	2	1	1	2	1	1	1	2	1	2	1	2
		Börjesson	1	2	1	1	2	2	2	2	2	2	2	1	2	1	1	1	1	3	4
		Rundblad	1	2	1	1	2	1	1	1	1	2	1	1	1	1	1	1	1	4	3
		Number of 2:s	0	3	0	0	0	2	2	3	2	2	2	1	0	1	2	1	2		
			33	19	14	13	12	26	39	36	37	38	38	47	17	33	47	52	47		

Candidate reliability +.05 +.39 −.08 +.28 +.79 +.36 −1 +.71 +.37 +.36 −.05 +.32 +.24 +.90 +.28 +.14 +.26 +.43
mean +.25

Nomination reliability +.24 +.66 +.06 +.59 +1 +.37 +.28 +.89 +.36 −.41 +.41 +.73 +.48 +1 +.30 +.99 +.61
mean +.51

This means evidently that the experts tend to use important categories sparingly and that they consider them so important that they use them according to their own conviction paying little regard to the opinion of the other experts. And so I use few 2:s and low reliability coefficients as indicators of the importance the experts attach to them.

Formulation and testing of hypotheses on the use of content analysis categories

I can use the reports of the experts to compare their use of categories as well as their evaluation of candidates. I believe that the trial lectures are given high priority as they measure "teaching ability", that the experts, evaluating the publications, pay most attention to the basic scientific categories and that they evaluate research publications and also researchers without regard for their department, scientific research area, etc. On this basis I formulate a number of hypotheses, summarized as hypothesis system A. The alternative hypothesis system B is based on the opposite idea.

Hypothesis system A then should mean that the evaluation of trial lectures is given the highest regard by experts as this category is the sole indicator on teaching ability (besides the faculty members have been present and the experts may be anxious to influence their opinion), the basic scientific categories should be given the next highest regard and so tend to have fewer 2:s and lower reliability coefficients than the remaining groups of categories. The additional scientific categories for similar reasons should be more important to the experts than the administrative categories.

Hypothesis system B then implies that the experts tend to pay most attention to the administrative factors and less attention to the remaining factors.

This leads to some alternative hypotheses:

Hypothesis A 1: The groups of categories should, ranked according to importance, measured as low numbers of 2:s, appear in the order: (1) Trial lectures, (2) Basic scientific categories, (3) Additional scientific categories, (4) Administrative categories.

Hypothesis B 1. The administrative categories should have more importance (lower mean of 2:s) than the other groups of categories.

Testing the hypotheses: The evaluation of the trial lectures have 16 2:s.

The basic scientific categories have 33, 19, 14, 13, 12 and 26 2:s.
Mean 20.
The additional scientific categories have 39, 36, 37, 38, 38 and 47 2:s.
Mean 40.
The administrative categories have 33, 47, 52. Mean 44.
Evidently I can reject hypothesis B 1.

Hypothesis A 2: The groups of categories should, ranked according to importance, measured as low reliability, appear in the order: (1) Trial lectures, (2) Basic scientific categories, (3) Additional scientific categories, (4) Administrative categories.

Hypothesis B 2: The administrative categories should have greater importance (lower reliability) than the other groups of categories.

Testing the hypotheses: The evaluation of trial lectures has the reliability -1.
The basic scientific categories have $+0.05$, $+0.36$, $+0.39$, -0.05, -0.08 and $+0.32$. Mean $+0.17$.
The additional scientific categories have $+0.28$, $+0.24$, $+0.79$, $+0.90$, -0.36, $+0.28$. Mean $+0.47$.
The administrative categories have $+0.14$, $+0.71$ and $+0.26$. Mean $+0.37$.

Testing the hypotheses: I reject hypothesis B 2, but I also have to reject a part of hypotheses A 2, as the additional scientific categories average higher in reliability than the administrative categories. That result depends on two categories: 9 (Number of books cited by the expert). The experts are rather careful to mention the few books and so the reliability of these categories is high: $+0.79$, $+0.90$. If they are omitted the data suit hypothesis A 2, which is wrong only on the relation between the additional and the administrative categories.

Hypothesis A 3. The experts have to evaluate each candidate in each case on the basis of their scientific production. Reliability then should be computed by comparisons of the three experts' reports on the same candidate. But instead of this "candidate" reliability it is possible to compute a "nomination" reliability by comparing the first place on the three nomination lists without regard to the candidate in that place, then the second place on the lists, and so on. As the experts' nomination lists differ from one another, this "nomination" reliability of course should be lower than the "candidate" reliability, comparing evaluations of the same researcher.

Hypothesis B 3. The experts are to prove to the faculty that their ranking of candidates on their nomination list is correct and so they tend to frame their evaluations in such a way that positive expressions go to the candidates at the top of their list, negative expressions to the bottom. Thus, the experts should agree more about the place on their nomination lists than about the candidates.

Testing the hypotheses: The reliability coefficients computed in these two ways are given below:

Category	Candidate reliability	Nomination reliability
1. Number of excellent publications	+0.05	+0.24
2. Number of innovations	+0.36	+0.36
3. Publications with good theory	+0.39	+0.66
4. Publications with good method	−0.05	−0.41
5. Publications designated as useful to society	−0.08	+0.06
6. The candidate's research trend	+0.32	+0.73
7. Number of publications cited by the expert	+0.28	+0.59
8. Number of research publications cited by the expert	+0.24	+0.48
9. Number of text books cited by the expert	+0.79	+1
10. Number of books cited by the expert	+0.90	+1
11. Candidate and expert have worked in the same field	+0.36	+0.37
12. The candidate probably can reciprocate the expert	+0.28	+0.30
13. The evaluation of the trial lecture	−1	+0.28
14. The candidate supposed to "suit" the faculty	+0.14	+0.99
15. The candidate's ability to cover the scope of the chair	+0.71	+0.89
16. The production of the candidate outside–inside the scope	+0.26	+0.61
Mean	+0.25	+0.50

Hypothesis A 3 must be rejected as candidate reliability is higher than nomination reliability only in one case, category 4.

The next phase of hypothesis construction refers either to differences between the candidates or to differences between the experts. The testing of hypothesis A 3 has shaken my confidence in the experts, but never the less I base system A on the assumption that the experts attend to scientific values more carefully than the faculty, where the members are to be given a new colleague to cooperate with and so may—consciously or unconsciously—pay more regard to their own interests. Such interests may already at the start of the procedure affect the choice of experts, excluding competent Swedish professors on behalf of professors in other

Scandinavian countries, who may be more favourable to a local candidate.

Hypothesis system B is based on the assumptions that the experts —consciously or unconsciously—try to expand their scientific empires by promoting their own men, while the faculty members are more anxious to secure the most competent candidates. Admittedly there are cases where A and B may be combined, but I have to neglect this possibility here. If an expert and a faculty do agree about the first name on the nomination list. I must interpret it as a scientifically sound decision, not as a successful plot. On this basis I formulate pairs of hypotheses:

Hypothesis A 4: In order to favor some candidate the faculty may select the experts so that a well qualified Swedish professor is excluded.

Hypothesis B 4: The faculty always selects the best available Swedish experts.

Testing the hypotheses: Who are the experts selected in our six cases? A scrutiny shows that hypothesis A 4 must be rejected. I hope that foreign readers will forgive my neglecting to present a whole page of a detailed and very tedious discussion.

Hypothesis A 5: The experts are so objective that they do not favor candidates from the faculty where the vacancy is to be filled, but tend to give them a lower place on the nomination list than the faculty does.

Hypothesis B 5: The experts do not give local candidates a lower place than the faculty does.

Testing the hypotheses: My 71 cases are accounted for in this table.

The candidate belongs to the faculty	The experts (compared with the faculty) give them		
	Higher rank	Same rank	Lower rank
With vacancy	8	18	8
Other faculty	8	21	8

These data show no bias. Hypothesis A 5 is rejected.

Hypothesis A 6: The experts do not favor candidates from their own department, whose work and weaknesses they tend to know and so tend to give them lower rankings on the nomination lists than the other experts.

Hypothesis B 6: The experts tend to give candidates from their own department higher rankings than the other experts, representing outside departments, do.

Testing the hypotheses: There are two cases, where an expert assigned a candidate from his own department a lower place than other experts, four cases where the experts did agree and six cases where an expert gave a higher place to a candidate from his own department. Hypothesis A 6 may be rejected.

Hypothesis A 7: The experts are more objective and informed than the faculty and so tend to give candidates from their own department a lower rank than the faculty does.

Hypothesis B 7: The experts do not tend to give candidates from their department a lower rank.

Testing the hypotheses: There is only one case where an expert assigned a candidate from his own department a lower place than the faculty did, four cases where experts and faculty did agree and two cases where the expert gave a candidate from his own department a higher place. Hypothesis A 7 is rejected.

Hypothesis A 8: The experts have enough objectivity and information to assign candidates from their own faculty (but outside their own department) lower places on the nomination list than the other experts do.

Hypothesis B 8: The experts do not assign candidates from their own faculty (but outside their own department) lower places than other experts do.

Testing the hypotheses: Seven cases give twelve comparisons. In three of the twelve the experts have given lower rank to candidates from their own faculty (but outside their own department), in six of them the experts did agree with one another and in three the experts have assigned the candidates from their own faculty the higher rank. Hypothesis A 8 is rejected.

Hypothesis A 9: The experts have enough objectivity and information to assign candidates from their own faculty lower places on the nomination list than the active faculty, where the vacancy is to be filled, does.

Hypothesis B 9: The experts do not assign candidates from their own faculty lower places than the active faculty, where the vacancy is to be filled.

Testing the hypotheses: Among seven relevant cases there is none where the expert has ranked a candidate from their own faculty lower than the active faculty, five cases where they agree and two cases where the expert has ranked such a candidate higher than the active faculty. Hypothesis A 9 may then be rejected.

I have allowed myself to reject the hypotheses A 3, A 4, A 5, A 6, A 7, A 8 and A 9 and with them this part of hypothesis system A, built on the objectivity and information of the experts. Hypothesis system B, built on the idea that the active faculty was more objective than the experts came out rather well. I postpone the discussion until I have formulated and tested the hypotheses based on Boalt's summation theory.

The summation theory applied to the reports of the experts

Until now I have not tried to relate the different content analysis categories to one another. How are the categories associated? I interpret positive evaluations in my categories as manifestations of scientific values and apply the summation theory as it is described in Boalt–Lantz–Ribbing: *Resources and Production of University Departments: Sweden and US* (Stockholm 1972, pp. 17 and 18). As the testing of hypotheses 10–13 indicate that it is an advantage to the candidates to belong to the same department and/or faculty as the expert I include these two categories, numbered 17 and 18 in my discussion of the summation theory: Some of my content analysis categories are by definition correlated to one another, as no. 9 (number of text books) with 10 (number of books including textbooks), or no. 2 (innovations) with 3 (publications with good, preferably new theory) and 4 (publications with good, preferably new method), 17 and 18. But in other cases categories may be correlated because they are based on the same trait in the candidates' production and/or the experts' evaluation system. Category 1 (excellent publications) then should be correlated with categories 2 (innovations), 3 (good theory) and 4 (good method) as these later categories must be used to justify the use of "Excellent publication". The content analysis categories in this way should split up in a number of clusters, each cluster made up of categories positively correlated with one another. But what about the correlations between categories from different clusters? That depends on the sample of candidates. If some of them are very good and some rather bad, the good candidates will tend to get high scores in all the categories and the poor candidates low scores and so all the correlations will tend to be positive. But if all candidates are pretty good, their specialization should show; some could for instance have high regard for theory and neglect method, others might prefer method and disregard theory. The clusters then come out clear-cut in a matrix, with positive correlations between categories in the same cluster and negative correlations between categories from different clusters, indicating that researchers may specialize in different directions, or that the experts are willing to forgive the theorists' mediocre methods and to forgive good methodologists their lack of theory. Such a matrix would show "a compensation pattern". But if mediocre and poor candidates slowly are added to the sample, the negative correlations between categories from different clusters slowly will be reduced and then turn positive, wiping out the lines between the clusters. A statistician might say that the matrix of a homogeneous sample of candidates is dominated by the variance within classes, a heterogeneous sample by the variance between classes.

My sample of candidates does of course not include very incompetent persons, but in some cases researchers not yet competent. I have then reasons to suspect that my total material will give a matrix with blurred clusters. To get more clear-cut clusters I have taken the two first names on each of my seventeen nomination lists from the experts. This matrix I will compare with the matrix from my total material and then—to test the summation theory on this point—with the matrix from a sample as heterogeneous as I can make it, taking the first and the last name from each of the seventeen nomination lists.

In these matrices it is useless to bring in categories, which by definition include one another and so I have excluded category 2 as it can be considered a sum of categories 3 and 4. Category 8 is covered by category 9 and so is excluded. Category 17 is covered by category 18, but 17 is more relevant and 18 then is excluded. Categories 11, 12, 15, 16 and 19 have to be excluded as their distribution is so skew among the first two candidates on the lists, that it is improper to use them for Q-coefficients. Only 15 categories are then left for the matrices.

I present and comment one matrix at a time and also discuss the outcome of the matrices according to the summation theory. The matrix of the correlations in the sample of the two best candidates on 17 lists is given in page 118. The categories have been arranged in such an order as to show the clusters.

Matrix of the correlations between 14 categories from the two foremost candidates on 17 nomination lists

	3	6	10	1	2	4	5	8	13	14	17	20	21	22
3. Publications with good theory	■	+.48	−.74	+.47	−.66	+.70	−.21	−.24	−.28	+.42	+.86	−.23	−.23	−.56
6. The candidate's research trend		■	−.30	−.50	−.37	+.48	−.45	−.74	−.81	+.20	−.42	−.74	−.69	−.26
10. Number of printed books			■	−.07	+.56	+.10	+.82	+.55	−.43	−.08	−.14	−.55	+.72	−.22
1. Number of excellent publications				■	+.74	+.04	+.68	+.57	+.05	+.67	+.62	+.63	+.36	+.44
2. Number of titles cited by the expert					■	+.23	+.44	+.83	+.53	−.26	+.39	+.51	−.12	±0
4. Publications with good method						■	−1	+.23	+.65	+1	+.61	+.27	+.27	−.59
5. Publications useful to society							■	+.68	+.13	+.40	+.20	+.68	+.68	−.34
8. Research publications cited by the expert								■	+.28	+.25	+.39	+.83	+.34	+.23
13. Evaluation of the trial lecture									■	+.04	+.11	+.53	±0	−.70
14. The candidate supposed to suit the faculty										■	+.05	+.45	+.95	−.63
17. The candidate and the expert from the same department											■	+.05	+.39	−1
20. Place on the expert's nomination lists												■	+.71	±0
21. Place on the faculty's nomination list													■	±0
22. Year of the case														■

Matrix *of the correlations between 14 categories from 71 reports of experts*

	3	6	10	1	2	4	5	8	13	14	17	20	21	22
3. Publications with good theory	■													
6. The candidate's research trend	+.46	■												
10. Number of printed books	−.06	−.65	■											
1. Number of excellent publications	+.82	+.76	+.11	■										
2. Number of titles cited by the expert	+.30	−.33	+.43	+.48	■									
4. Publications with good method	+.65	+.28	+.27	+.74	+.15	■								
5. Publications useful to society	+.29	−.02	+.43	+.64	+.43	+.41	■							
8. Research publications cited by the expert	+.62	+.37	+.51	+.43	+.85	+.35	+.26	■						
13. Evaluation of the trial lecture	+.51	−.05	−.35	+.51	+.41	+.65	−.06	+.54	■					
14. The candidate supposed to suit the faculty	+.64	+.48	−.16	+.64	+.30	+.54	+.35	−.17	+.85	■				
17. The candidate and the expert from the same department	+.42	+.03	+.06	+.61	−.22	+.21	+.36	−.11	+.45	+.11	■			
20. Place on the expert's nomination list	+.87	+.39	+.38	+.87	+.35	+.11	+.65	+.41	+.62	+.45	+.80	■		
21. Place on the faculty's nomination list	+.71	+.65	+.21	+.71	+.14	+.47	+.65	+.41	+.62	+.77	+.30	+.92	■	
22. Year of the case	+.64	−.56	+.54	+.08	−.04	+.22	+.48	+.19	−.72	+.07	−.47	+.02	+.02	■

The matrix page 118 presents three clusters of content analysis categories. The first can be labelled the "theoretical" cluster as it contains category 3, publications with good or new theory, and category 6, a rising research trend. The second cluster is made up only of category 10, number of printed books. The third cluster contains the remaining six content analysis categories (1, 2, 4, 5, 8 and 13) and we label it the "method and merit" cluster. Outside the content analysis categories the administrative and nomination categories 14, 17, 20 and 21 join the "method and merit" cluster, but the candidates from the later cases (after 1967, category 22) are lower (or evaluated lower) in all categories but excellent publications (category 1) and number of cited research reports (category 8).

How clear-cut are the three clusters? The first "theoretical" cluster has a correlation +0.48 between its two categories, two negative correlations out of two with the second cluster and nine negative correlations out of twelve with the categories in the third. The first cluster, thus is rather well separated from the others. Not so the second. The number of printed books have only two negative correlations out of six with the categories in the third, "method and merit" cluster, but tends to have negative correlations with the "administrative and nomination" categories connected with the third cluster and so can be kept separate. If we unite the four administrative categories 14, 17, 20 and 21 with the method and merit cluster, it contains ten categories with forty-five intercorrelations only two of them negative.

I interpret this pattern as an indication that theoretically oriented candidates have little regard for book production, many publications, usefulness to society, do not perform trial lectures well, often have some affiliation to the faculty but tend to get low rank on the nomination lists. Candidates with a large printed production try to be useful to society and are ranked high by the faculty. Candidates covering the categories in the "method and merit" cluster tend to be given the first place in the nomination lists. But these tendencies may more or less be the result of the experts' formulation.

I now turn to the correlation matrix from my total sample of 71 reports and then use the clusters from the previous matrix, hoping to find some marks of them in the new matrix in page 119.

The matrix from all the 71 reports actually no longer can be said to have clear clusters as there are only 15 negative correlations out of 81, but 11 of them belong to the 45 correlations between categories from different clusters, only 4 to the 46 correlations between categories in same cluster. There are, thus, still some traces of the clear-cut clusters from my first matrix. This result suits the summation theory very well.

It is interesting to note that in this sample the experts seem to pay most regard to good and/or new theory (category 3, +0.87), excellent publications (category 1, +0.87) and to candidates from their own department (category 17, +0.80). The faculty on the other hand seems, very properly, to be influenced more by the experts' reports (category 20, +0.92), than by the category "candidate supposed to suit the faculty", but this category is very difficult to estimate (the correlation +0.77 may easily be the effect of the faculty's decision instead of a cause to it), but the categories 1 and 3 have a strong correlation not only with the ranking in the experts' nomination lists but also in those of the faculties. But please remember that the experts as full professors have a considerable experience of how reports are handled by faculties and so tend to follow the successful patterns in their reports. I must stress here that I analyse the content of the *experts' reports*, not the content of the *candidates' publications*.

My last correlation matrix is from the most heterogeneous sample: the first and the last on the experts' nomination lists. It is presented in the next page. I have here omitted categories 20 and 21 (the ranking of the candidates in the nomination lists) as these categories have been used to select the sample and so would generally give perfect correlations with the content analysis categories. See matrix in page 122.

This matrix contains only two negative correlations and so all the categories seem to form one single cluster. The two negative correlations both belong, however, to the 26 correlations between categories from different clusters in my first matrix and so are the last remnants of the clustering.

When I compare my three matrices I restrict myself to the nine content analysis categories. I expected more clear-cut clusters in the first matrix with small differences between the candidates, blurred clusters in the second matrix from my total material and hardly any clusters at all in the third matrix. I express these expectations as a single hypothesis, but I cannot use the first matrix to test hypotheses about the clusters, as these have been defined so as to give the best possible clusters in the first matrix.

Hypothesis 10. The second matrix should have more negative correlations between content analysis categories from different clusters than the

Matrix *of the correlations between 11 categories from the first and the last candidates on 17 nomination lists*

	3	6	10	1	2	4	5	8	13	14	17	20	21
3. Publications with good theory	■	+.29	+.42	+1	+1	+.70	+.52	+1	+1	+.54	+.22	×	×
6. The candidate's research trend		■	+.20	+1	±0	+.79	+.70	−.48	+1	+1	−1	×	×
10. Number of printed books			■	+.69	+.24	+.76	+.39	+.46	+.86	+.50	+.43	×	×
1. Number of excellent publications				■	+.55	+1	+.74	+.38	+.86	+.76	+.57	×	×
2. Number of titles cited by the expert					■	+.66	+.79	+.98	+.79	+.25	+.66	×	×
4. Publications with good method						■	+.52	+.36	+1	+.54	+.20	×	×
5. Publications useful to society							■	+.62	+1	+.09	+.95	×	×
8. Research publications cited by the expert								■	+.88	+.32	+.74	×	×
13. Evaluation of the trial lecture									■	+.80	+1	×	×
14. The candidate supposed to "suit" the faculty										■	+.54	×.	×
17. The candidate and the expert from the same department											■	×	×
20. First place on the expert's nomination												■	×
21. Place on the faculty's nomination list													■

third matrix. Testing the hypothesis: The negative correlations between categories from different clusters are 13 in the first matrix, 6 in the second and 2 in the third. The hypothesis then can not be rejected in this case, which is in favor of the summation theory.

Discussion

I made from the start a classification of the categories in five groups and predicted the importance the experts would attach to each group. The prediction turned out comparatively well.

My application of the summation theory to the interaction of the content analysis factors has given interesting results, but the theory cannot be used to decide to which extent the demonstrated clusters of categories mirror trends in the candidates' publications and to which extent they are the results of the experts' technique for phrasing their reports.

My most important result is the fact that the experts agree better on how to use the categories to evaluate the places on their nomination lists than on how to evaluate individual candidates. Why? The simplest explanation is that they tend to use standard formulations to justify their ranking of the candidates. I believe that this is not the truth—or at least not the whole truth. Content analysis has drawbacks and may be misleading in this case. I take category 3, good and/or new theory, as an example. To say that a candidate has presented such a theory is to pay him a very high compliment—and to take a considerable risk. Suppose the theory is rather well known, but not known to the expert. That would prove that the expert is no expert. And so he has to use such categories sparingly. But he does use it to some extent in unexpected cases, such as "the investigation is badly planned and the material not very relevant to the problem, but I admit that the theory is interesting and probably new". Similar cases happen to category 6, the candidates research trend. A rising research trend should be a high complement, but can easily be used to sugar a bitter pill: "The candidate's later publications are, however, on a higher level" etc. Poor candidates have, after all, far greater chance to improve than very good ones. But this technique to use one category to compensate the shortcomings in another is hardly possible to analyse with my simple categories. I have to accept, that some categories may show low reliability as the experts tend to use them for sugar-coating in very different cases. This would result in more variations when different experts evaluate the same candidate, whose rank they disagree about than when the experts evaluate the top places on their nomination lists where they need not use sugar-coating and the bottom places, where sugar-coating should be needed more often. I am, thus, inclined not to take the differences between nomination reliability and candidate reliability too seriously. But how do faculty members and candidates react to the experts' subtle use of the evaluation phrases for sugaring some bitter pills? Well, faculty members, of course, can pick out a number of such phrases in order to prove the superiority of a special candidate, which of course annoys not only the expert, who has himself to blame, but also his foremost candidate. The bottom candidates are meant to get some consolation out of the sugar, but it might also give them too much confidence in their ability. The top candidates may react in the opposite direction: "Why does this expert pay high compliments to bad candidates and not to me? He has a bias against me, although my merits are so high that he is unable to skip me." And so the sugaring technique may cause barriers to rise between the experts and the faculty members as well as between the experts and the new professors they have helped along to their chairs.

I suspect that the two categories 3 and 6 (especially 6), which I have taken as examples, are often used to compensate shortcomings in other categories. If so this could to some extent explain why these two categories form a cluster of their own in my first matrix and still have negative correlations with some categories in the second matrix. But on the other hand I believe that candidates with a gift for theory tend to be less interested in methodology, etc. But I admit that my data cannot tell, whether the clusters in the matrices have a basis in the publications and merits of the candidates or if they only are artefacts based on the reporting technique of the experts. I guess that there is a lot in both explanations, although the cluster made up of category 10 (number of printed books) hardly can be artefact.

I have hardly discussed category 22, the year of the case. The student troubles in 1967 and 1968 gave emphasis to Marxist theory, that is, to categories 4 (good or new theory) and 5 (publications useful to society). My matrix of all the 71 reports shows that the categories used more often after 1967 are category 3 (good or new theory) with a correlation $+0.64$, category 5 (publications useful to society) with $+0.48$, category 4 (good or new methods) with $+0.22$, while the remaining categories have associations below $+0.20$ or negative. This can be interpreted as an indication that research and/or the experts' evaluations have been influenced by the shift toward radicalism. If so, this shift might create a barrier between the older, less radical professors and the younger, more radical.

Chapter 10

Generation differences among researchers and teachers in a Sociological department

Gunnar Boalt and Ulla Bergryd

We use our own department of Sociology at the University of Stockholm for this study, as we know far more about it than about any other. Regular teaching in Sociology started here in 1949, but the department at the University in Uppsala had been organized two years earlier. At Uppsala the sociologists soon developed an interest in theoretical sociology (the Uppsala school of sociology) but at Stockholm the sociologists preferred empirical, descriptive studies, paying far more attention to methods than to theory. As practically all the teachers in the subject had this non-theoretical orientation it soon became a part of the research pattern at Stockholm and influenced the teaching as well. This pattern could not remain unchanged, however. As the department expanded, several young members went to universities in the United States and brought back very different ideas, clearly reflected also in the dominating, international journals, but teaching still followed the traditional lines when the students in 1968 began to protest against university administration, teaching, textbooks, etc. Radical sociology students wanted theory, also radical theory, with Marx and Mao on the reading lists, and when the students acquired formal representation at the department board, the lists were changed accordingly.

The teaching pattern could be changed this way, but to change the research pattern was far more difficult and will take far more time. The established researchers did seldom change their ways. The young researchers' dissertation work was planned long ago and had to follow the plans. Young radical students gave a good deal of attention to students politics, that may have taken some time from research. But the best students now tended to be radical and from them the fresh assistants were recruited. After some time they made or may make their M.A. (licentiatexamen) and eventually a Ph.D.

In our opinion there may be a generation gap at the department between an older, descriptive, methodological, non-theoretical research pattern and a new, radical, more theoretical research pattern. But we must point out that if there is a gap, there probably also is an overlapping. Some of the young teachers and researchers had already before 1968—at their peril—taken an interest in theoretical sociology and some were quite radical for those days. In the same way some new researchers and/or teachers may still accept the methodologically oriented non-theoretical research pattern etc. and thus use the set of professors as their reference-groups, not their fellow-students.

But professors still occupy important positions at Swedish university departments. They do not decide the content of courses, the choice of textbooks or the selection of teaching assistants, but they do decide the marks of M.A. theses and dissertations, they do influence research-grants and the selection of associate and full professors is practically in their hands. How do they react in these cases to candidates using their own research patterns and to candidates using another, more radical one?

That is our problem. Four different materials have been used:

1. In order to study marks, publications and research career Bjurman, Bohm and Boalt have collected data on the 67 sociologists who have attained the old M.A. degree (licentiatexamen) at the university of Stockholm.
2. In order to study selection and career of the teachers Bjurman has collected data on 26 teachers with M.A., teaching sociology at the department in 1972.
3. Similarly we made a less ambitious study of 79 junior teachers without tenure at the department in 1967–1972 in order to study the hiring and firing procedures, etc.
4. As the full professors are few but placed in key positions, Bergryd made a study of the experts' written recommendations, which form the basis for the selection of candidates to professional chairs.

The results from these studies are reported in the three previous chapters and do not contradict our expectations built on the summation theory. Are there any data indicating generation gaps or contrasts between traditional and radical research patterns? Bjurman's study of the 67 researchers pointed out that those graduated (M.A.) in the 'seventies, tended to have a higher level of aspiration as far as theory was concerned. They are, however, few and can hardly influence the general pattern of all 67. If we want to know anything about this group, we have to separate them from the rest, compute the correlation between the traits in this particular sample and see if their correlation matrix contains clusters according to our expectations.

Turning our attention to differences between teachers, Bjurman's as well as Bohm's studies of the 26 teachers assign the generation factor, years in the department, to a cluster of its own, but when the sample is divided in two samples, good teachers and less good teachers, the generation factor no longer joins the deviating clusters in these new matrices. In our opinion this indicates that teachers may compensate other merits with years at the department, but if the teachers are divided in good ones and not so good ones, years at the department are less useful to compensate other traits and so they are—in spite of some negative correlations with the traits of general merits—included in this large cluster. If we want more information on differences in research patterns between conservative and radical teachers, we have to divide our sample of 26 teachers in 13 more conservative and 13 more radical ones and find out what their correlation matrices have to tell.

We start with the 12 sociologists graduated after 1969. We expect some of them to cling to traditional research values and others to pay less attention to them. Contacts with the professor may on the one side indicate acceptance of his traditional values, on the other need of his help with research problems. We thus expect one cluster of traditional research values and another cluster somehow opposed to it, while professorial contacts may side up with the first cluster, if professors mainly act as preservers of traditional values, but with the second if they mainly have to support M.A. candidates in distress.

The matrix is given in page 128. It contains three, quite clear clusters: the large traditional cluster, made up of 13 variables (1, 2, 3, 4, 5, 7, 8, 9, 13, 14, 16, 17, 18), another cluster of three variables (6, level of aspiration to methodology; 11, status with the professor and 12, personal contact with the professor) and at last an unexpected little cluster made of male sex (15).

This indicates that the young bright set after all sticks to traditional research values, but do not take them through their contacts with professors, who seem to be dominated by their role as supporters of weak M.A. candidates, supervising at least their methodology. The men in the sam-

Matrix 1. *Matrix of the correlations from a sample of 12 sociologists, M.A. after 1969*

	2	3	4	5	7	8	9	13	14	16	17	18	6	11	12	15
1. Ego-strength	+1	+1	+.80	+.25	+.75	+1	+.80	+1	+1	+.40	+.40	+1	±0	+1	±0	-.50
2. Independence, subject		+.90	+1	+1	+.60	+1	+.20	+1	+1	+.80	+.80	+1	-1	-1	-1	-.40
3. Independence, method			+1	+1	+1	+1	+1	+1	+1	+.80	+.80	+1	+.60	+1	±0	-.40
4. Perseverance				+.68	+.60	+1	+.06	+1	+1	+1	+1	+1	-.23	+1	+.33	-.80
5. Level of aspiration. Theory					+1	+1	+.68	+1	+1	+1	+1	+1	+1	+1	-.82	-.50
7. Innovation						+1	+1	+1	+1	+.60	+1	+1	+.88	+1	+1	±0
8. Status outside the department							+1	+1	+1	+1	+1	+1	-1	-1	-1	+1
9. Status in peer-group								+1	+1	+.20	+.20	+1	+.90	+1	-.33	+.50
13. Marks in M.A... etc.									+1	+1	+1	+1	-1	+1	-1	+1
14. Printed production										+1	+1	+1	-1	-1	±0	+1
16. Choice of career											+1	+1	-1	-1	±0	-.40
17. Appointment in sociology												+1	-1	-1	-1	-.40
18. Appointment at Stockholm dep.													+1	+1	-1	+1
6. Level of aspiration. Method														+1	-.43	±0
11. Status among professors															+1	-1
12. Personal contact professors																±0
15. Male sex																

ple have high status outside the department and in their peer-group, high marks and good scientific production, but otherwise they tend to pay less attention than the female researchers to the traits in the two clusters.

From the professors' point of view this picture is rather sad. It means that they tend to get isolated from the young generation of researchers, who do not badly need their help. If so the generation gap will increase.

Let us then turn to the 26 teachers at the sociology department and divide them in a radical and a non-radical group, according to Bjurman's classification. We believe there is a considerable over-lap in research technique, between the two groups, as many of the radical sociologists started teaching long ago and have not changed their approach since then. We expect the scientific values to form a cluster together with career variables and some of the teaching variables, while other teaching traits form an alternate cluster.

The matrix in page 130 presents us with two clusters, one large cluster containing all scientific and career variables together with most of those covering the teaching (variables 2, 3, 4, 5, 6, 7, 8, 9, 10, 11, 12, 13, 14, 16, 18, 21, 27, 28 and 29). The second, smaller cluster contains three variables: ego-strength (1), level of aspiration for own teaching (24) and production of teaching material (26). This indicates that radical teachers with good scientific merits tend to have less ego strength, lower level of aspiration for their own teaching and to produce less material for the teaching. But radical teachers, less burdened with scientific merits, tend to have strong ego and pay more attention to their own teaching and production of teaching materials.

Bjurman's matrix for all 26 teachers indicated reasonable contacts between radical teachers and professors. This seems to contradict our previous opinion on the generation gap. Yes, but teachers are only a part of the M.A.s and there is, after all, a far greater chance to keep contacts between the teachers in one department. Our data in the matrix page 130 seem to indicate that the generation gap is smaller between professors and the research minded teachers than between professors and the ego strong teachers producing material for the teaching. Well that may be bad, but in our opinion it would be far worse if the professors had lost the contact with the radical, research-minded teachers.

We proceed to the matrix of the correlations from the sample of 13 non-radical teachers. As these non-radical teachers from several points of view over-lap with the radical ones, we believe that the clusters for

Matrix 2. Correlations from a sample of 13 radical teachers, M.A.

	2	3	4	5	6	7	8	9	10	11	12	13	14	16	18	20	21	27	28	29	1	24	26
2. Independence, subject	+1	+.60	+.43	+1	+.43	+.60	+1	+.41	+1	+.73	−.41	+.93	+.93	+.85	+.93	+.73	+1	+.41	+.14	+.20	+1	+.43	+.20
3. Independence, method		+1	+.85	+1	+.14	+.85	+1	+.71	+1	+.94	+.58	+.74	+1	+.85	+1	+.67	+1	+.71	+.50	+.67	+1	+.45	−.45
4. Perseverance			+1	+.85	+.43	+.85	+.73	+.83	+1	+.85	+1	+1	+1	+1	+1	+.43	+1	+.82	+.65	+.43	+.93	+.20	−.20
5. Level of aspiration. Theory				+1	+.27	+.85	+1	+.71	+1	+.85	+1	+1	+1	+1	+1	+1	+1	+1	+.64	+.09	+1	+1	+1
6. Level of aspiration. Method					+1	+1	+1	+.64	+.50	+.67	−.11	+.20	+.20	+.45	+.20	+.14	+.64	+1	+.64	+.14	+1	+.45	+.67
7. Innovation						+1	+.83	+.71	+.50	+1	+.41	−.11	+.20	+.20	+.14	+.50	+.50	+.14	+.43	+.74	+.45	+.43
8. Status outside the department							+1	+.74	+1	+.85	+.41	+1	+1	+.94	+1	+.85	+.85	+.33	+.65	+.14	+.43
9. Status in peer-group								+1	+.58	+.71	+.11	+1	+1	+1	+1	+.94	+1	+.92	+.78	+.45	+.58	+.11
10. Status among students									+1	+.78	−.20	+1	+1	+1	+1	+1	+1	+.08	−1	+.50	+1	+.50
11. Status among professors										+1	+.58	+.73	+1	+1	+1	+.50	+1	+.71	+.50	+.93	+.45	+.11
12. Personal contacts with professors											+1	+.73	+.73	+.85	+.73	+.67	+1	+.20	−.08	+.58	+.58	+.50
13. Marks in M.A... etc.												+1	+.33	+.11	+.33	+1	+1	+1	+1	+.93	+.20	+.14
14. Printed production													+1	+1	+1	+1	+1	+1	+1	+.20	−.20	−.43
16. Choice of career														+1	+1	+.85	+1	+.71	+.50	+.14	+.45	−.43
18. Higher appointment															+1	+.73	+1	+1	+1	+.20	+.20	−.71
20. Academic level of teaching																+1	+.93	+.94	+.92	+.20	+.45	+.14
21. Ability to teach																	+1	+.71	+1	+.14	+.45	+.50
27. Interest in teaching																		+1	+.07	+.11	−.67	−.45
28. Interest in theoretical items																			+1	+.50	−.50	−.33
29. Years in department																				+.20	−.14	−.45
1. Ego-strength																					+1	+.20	+.43
24. Level of aspiration for own teaching																						+1	+.43
26. Production of teaching material																							+1

these two samples show similarities. We thus expect a dominating research and career cluster including some teaching values and then another cluster made up of other teaching variables, probably including some of the variables (1, 24 and 26) which made up the second cluster among the radical teachers.

The matrix is presented in page 132. It contains three clusters: the large research and career cluster (2, 3, 4, 5, 6, 7, 8, 9, 11, 12, 13, 14, 16, 18, 20 and 29) we expected, a second cluster of six variables (1, ego-strength; 10, status among students; 21, ability for teaching; 24, level of aspiration for own teaching; 26, production of teaching material; 27, interest in teaching) and a third small cluster made up only of 28, interest in the theoretical items.

The first large cluster contains, as we expected, all the traditional research values and career variables together with good promotion (18), teaching at higher levels (20) and years at the department (29). The second cluster contained 6 variables, among them 1, 24 and 26, which formed the second cluster in matrix 2. It is interesting that these have been joined by status among students (10), ability for teaching (21) and interest in teaching (27). This suggests that the traditional research merits among the non-radical teachers may be compensated by traits including ego-strength, status among students, ability for and interest in teaching etc. Those teachers who neither have research merits, nor teaching merits may take the chance to compensate this by overdoing their interest for the theoretical items in their teaching.

There is no visible generation gap between professors and non-radical teachers going in for research and research merits. There seems, however, to be a gap between professors and non-radical teachers specializing in teaching or going in for theoretical points. This is no surprise.

Summing up the indications on generation gaps, we have found that the last batch of M.A.s, graduating after 1969, do accept traditional research values and yet have little contact with professors; that is, these contacts tend to be restricted to weak M.A. candidates, who need help (esp. with methods) when their research gets stuck. But among the teachers, whether they are radical or not, those who have research merits also tend to keep in contact with the professor. This seems to be a contradiction. We must, however, point out that a strong majority of the teachers, 16 out of 26, have taken their M.A. degree before 1970 and probably followed the patterns of all 67 researchers, where the correlation matrix showed a single large cluster containing not only research values but also contacts with the professor.

Matrix 3. Correlations from a sample of 13 non-radical teachers

	3	4	5	6	7	8	9	11	12	13	14	16	18	20	29	1	10	21	24	26	27	28
2. Independence, subject	+.83	+.33	+.27	+.85	+.64	+.64	+.64	+.43	−.05	+.93	+.93	+.35	+.33	+.83	+.43	−.14	−.14	−1	−.43	−1	−1	−.14
3. Independence, method		+.92	+.45	+1	+.83	+.83	+.33	+.71	−.33	+.83	+.83	+1	+.92	+.56	+.11	−1	−.20	+.78	+.58	−.58	−.58	+.08
4. Perseverance			+.45	+1	+1	+.83	+.83	+1	+.41	+.83	+.83	+1	+.92	+.92	+.11	−1	+.08	+.08	+.58	−.58	−.28	−1
5. Level of aspiration. Theory				+.45	+.69	+.27	+.27	+1	+1	+.27	+.27	+.89	−1	+.45	−1	+.64	+1	+.64	+1	+.09	−1	−1
6. Level of aspiration. Method					+1	+.27	+.85	+.24	+.20	+1	+1	+1	+1	+1	+.14	−.33	−.33	−.33	−.14	−.92	−.58	−.33
7. Innovation						+1	+.93	+1	+.60	+.93	+.93	+1	+1	+1	+.43	−.14	−.14	−.14	+.20	−.74	−.41	−1
8. Status outside the department							+.93	+.85	−.05	+.95	+.95	+1	+.83	+.83	−.20	−.14	−.14	−.14	+.43	−.74	−.41	−.14
9. Status in peer-group								+.85	+1	+.94	+.94	+.85	+.83	+.83	−.20	+.65	+.65	+.65	+.20	−.73	−.41	−.14
11. Status among professors									+.85	+.85	+.85	+.94	+1	+1	+.14	+.50	+.50	+.50	+.45	−.45	−.60	−1
12. Personal contact with profes-sors										+.60	+.60	+.20	+.41	+1	−.85	+1	+1	+1	−.20	+.20	−.33	−.58
13. Marks in M.A..etc.											+1	+1	+.83	+1	−.20	−.14	−.14	−.14	−.43	−1	−1	−.14
14. Printed production												+1	+.83	+1	−.20	−.14	−.14	−.14	−.43	−1	−1	−.14
16. Choice of career													+1	+.71	+.14	−.33	−.33	−.33	−.33	−.85	+.58	−.33
18. Higher appointment														+.92	+.71	+.08	−1	+.08	−.11	−.58	−.20	−1
20. Academic level of teaching															+.11	+.08	+.08	+.14	−.10	−1	−1	−1
29. Years in department																−.33	−.33	−1	+.45	−.45	+.11	−.33
1. Ego-strength																	+.90	+.90	+.33	+.50	+.08	−1
10. Status among students																		+.90	+1	+.50	−.08	−1
21. Ability to teach																			+.33	+.50	+.08	−1
24. Level of aspiration for own teaching																				+.45	+.33	+.50
26. Production of teaching material																					+1	+.50
27. Interest in teaching																						+.78
28. Interest in theoretical items																						

We can test this idea in a very simple way, comparing the data on status according to the professor (11) and contacts with him (12) on the 16 teachers, graduated before 1970, with the 10 teachers graduated after 1969:

	Strength on a 5 point scale					
	1	2	3	4	5	Mean
11. *Status according to the professor*						
16 teachers, graduated before 1970	–	3	1	6	6	3.9
10 teachers, graduated after 1969	1	1	7	1	–	2.8
12. *Personal contacts with the professor*						
16 teachers, graduated before 1970	–	2	7	3	4	3.6
10 teachers, graduated after 1969	1	2	2	4	1	3.2

The older teachers do have higher status and more contacts with the professor—as we expected.

This contradiction thus might be viewed as a contrast between an older research pattern, without a generation gap between researchers and professors, and a recent pattern with such a gap. This new gap may be the result of a changed research ideology, but, of course the generation gap also tends to widen because professors do grow older and new students do not.

Kerstin Bohm has in her chapter mentioned that the department is divided in two large groups, 10 teachers who have their office on the 8th floor of the B-house and 16 who have theirs at the 9th. From the start, there probably was some tendency to locate full professors to the 9th floor, assistants and project staffs to the 8th, but as full professors in charge of projects wanted to be near their staff, some of them got offices on the 8th adjoining their research staffs. This led to some reshuffling, but now, three years afterwards, everybody seems anxious to remain at his floor and there is far more interaction within the floors than between them. The floors then might serve as reference-groups, transmitting research and/or teaching patterns.

If the floors tend to have different patterns, this could hardly be interpreted as a generation barrier, located in the flooring between them, but it could be something of a geographical or ecological barrier to communication on the micro level. The research patterns generally have remained rather stable among the graduated teachers, we can hardly expect the flooring to influence that, but the teaching pattern has changed far more and might show differences. We have tried this idea and worked out correlation matrices for the two floors. They are presented as matrices 4 and 5 on pages 135 and 136.

Matrix 4, page 135, sums up our data on the 10 teachers on the 8th floor. All research and teaching variables tend to be positively correlated and so there is only one single cluster with 18 negative correlations out of 276, that is 7%. Variables 29, 27 and 12 are responsible for most of the negative correlations, but there are too few to justify an aberrant cluster.

Matrix 5, page 136, presents the correlations in the sample of 16 teachers on the 9th floor. It has three different clusters instead of one. There is a large cluster containing all research variables and career variables, including 20, academic level of teaching and 21, ability to teach. There is a second cluster, made up of five teaching variables: 23, radicalism, 24, level of aspiration for own teaching, 25, production of teaching material, 27, interest in teaching and 28, interest in the theoretical items. The last cluster contains one single variable: 29, years in the department.

This is interesting. The two floors do not differ in research pattern, but they do differ very much in teaching pattern. Teachers from the 8th floor tend to be good teachers if they have attained high research values, but teachers from the 9th floor tend to attain low teaching values if they have high research ones.

The textbooks and the courses have recently been made more radical. It seems as if the teachers on the 8th floor have been able to adapt to this change. Among them radicalism (variable 23) is correlated with research variables as well as with teaching variables. But the teachers on the 9th floor, who have good research data, tend to keep a distance not only from radicalism but also from most other teaching values. The most important teaching variable, 21, ability to teach, is, however, positively correlated with the research values as well as with teaching variables. Variable 29, years at the department, tends to be negatively correlated with research as well as with teaching.

There are, thus, the same research pattern but very different teaching patterns on the two floors. This must not be interpreted as a pure group-effect. The original selection probably meant a great deal. But once this difference was established by selection, it probably has been considerably strengthened by interaction within each floor and by a tendency to isolation between them. Selection, interaction and isolation

Matrix 4. Correlations from a sample of 10 teachers at the 8th floor

	2	3	4	5	6	7	8	9	10	11	12	13	14	16	18	20	21	23	24	26	27	28	29
1. Ego-strength	+.45	+.88	+1	+1	+.88	+1	+1	+1	+1	+.88	+.48	+.71	+.71	+.88	+.71	+.88	+1	+1	+1	+1	+.71	+1	+.45
2. Independence, subject		+.88	+1	+.20	+.45	+.45	+.85	+1	−.11	+.45	−.20	+1	+1	+1	+1	+1	−.20	−.11	+1	+1	−.67	−.11	−.11
3. Independence, method			+1	+.71	+.45	+.88	+1	+1	+.45	+.88	+.71	+1	+1	+.85	+1	+.88	+.71	+.45	+1	+1	±0	+.45	+.45
4. Perseverance				+.67	+1	+1	+1	+.85	+.85	+1	+1	+1	+1	+.71	+.67	+.71	+1	+.85	+.88	+.85	+.67	+.67	+.11
5. Level of aspiration. Theory					+.71	+.71	+1	+1	+1	+.85	−.33	+.67	+.67	+.71	+.67	+.71	+1	+1	+1	+.88	+.88	+1	−.20
6. Level of aspiration. Method						+1	+1	+1	+.45	+1	+.71	+.71	+.71	+.88	+.71	+.88	+.71	+.45	+1	+1	+.71	+.45	+1
7. Innovation							+.45	+1	+.67	+.67	+.67	+1	+1	+1	+1	+1	+1	+.67	+1	+1	+.33	+.67	+.67
8. Status outside dep.								+1	+1	+1	−.20	+1	+1	+1	+1	+1	+.67	+1	+1	+1	+.20	+1	−.11
9. Status in peer-group									+.85	+.45	−.20	+1	+1	+1	+1	+.45	+1	+.85	+1	+.85	+.67	+.82	+.11
10. Status among students										+.45	+.20	+.20	+1	+.45	+.20	+.45	+1	+1	+1	+1	±.67	+.85	−
11. Status among professors											+.71	+.71	+.71	+.45	+.71	+.88	+.71	+.45	+1	+1	±0	+.45	+1
12. Personal contact professors												+.33	+.33	+0	+.33	+.33	+.33	+.20	+.20	+.20	−.33	+.20	+.20
13. Marks in M.A.., etc.													+1	+1	+1	+1	+1	+.20	+1	+1	−.33	+.20	+.20
14. Printed production														+1	+1	+1	+.71	+.45	+1	+1	±0	+.20	+.45
16. Choice of career															+1	+1	+.71	+.20	+1	+1	±0	+.45	+.45
18. Higher appointment																+1	+.33	+.20	+1	+1	−.33	+.20	+.20
20. Academic level of teaching																	+.71	+.45	+1	+1	0	+.45	+.45
21. Ability to teach																		+1	+1	+.66	+.66	+1	+.20
23. Radicalism																			+.85	+.85	+1	+.85	−1
24. Level of aspiration for own teaching																				+1	+.67	+.67	+.11
26. Production of teaching material																					+.67	+.85	+.11
27. Interest in teaching																						+.67	−1
28. Interest in theoretical items																							+.11
29. Years in department																							

Matrix 5. Correlations from a sample of 16 teachers at the 9th floor

	2	3	4	5	6	7	8	9	10	11	12	13	14	16	18	20	21	23	24	26	27	28	29
1. Ego-strength	+.65	+.40	+.08	+.65	−.50	+.20	+.50	+.50	+.78	+.84	+.50	+.40	+.40	+.20	+.60	+.40	+.76	+.40	+.40	+.40	+.90	−.14	+.40
2. Independence, subject		+.90	+.56	+.45	+.45	+.56	+.90	+.45	+.65	+.67	−.25	+.91	+.90	+.80	+.45	+.65	+.08	−.33	+.20	−.33	−.03	+.20	+.65
3. Independence, method			+1	+.20	+.84	+.90	+1	+.90	+.78	+.84	±0	+.95	+.95	+1	+.78	+.78	+.76	+.40	+.40	+.40	+.20	+.40	−.14
4. Perserverance				+.45	+.75	+1	+1	+.83	+.60	+1	+.29	+.90	+.92	+1	+.98	+.91	+.65	−.08	+.08	+.08	−.11	+.08	+.08
5. Level of aspiration. Theory					+.25	+.45	+.25	+.45	+1	+.67	−.25	+.20	+.20	−.08	−.11	+.65	+.85	+.65	+.65	−.33	−.33	+.20	−.33
6. Level of aspiration. Method						+.95	+.80	+.67	±0	+.47	−.47	+.84	+.85	+.01	+.76	+.85	−.25	±0	±0	−.50	−.91	−.50	−.50
7. Innovation							+.95	+.80	+.85	+.91	+.25	+.91	+.90	+.96	+1	+1	+.62	+.20	+.20	−.33	−.52	0	+.20
8. Status outside dep.								+.91	+.96	+.91	+.25	+.91	+1	+1	+1	+1	±0	−.50	+.20	−.50	−.25	0	+.50
9. Status in peer-group									+.67	+.96	±0	+1	+1	+1	+1	+.85	+.62	+.20	+.20	−.33	0	−.25	+.20
10. Status among students										+.65	+.65	+.85	+.85	+.80	+.76	+.85	±0	−.50	−.50	−.33	±0	−.25	+.50
11. Status among professors											+1	±0	+1	+1	+1	+.85	+.52	+.65	+.65	−.14	−.03	−.33	−.33
12. Personal contact professor												+.47	+.50	+.25	+.29	+.50	+.25	±0	±0	−.50	+.25	−.50	−.50
13. Marks in M.A., etc.													+.50	+.25	+.29	+.50	+.25	−.50	−.50	−.50	−.50	−.50	−.50
14. Printed production														+1	+.89	+.96	−.20	−.14	−.14	−.67	−.14	+.40	−.50
16. Choice of career															+1	+.96	+.96	−.33	−.14	−.14	−.14	−.40	−.14
18. Higher appointment																+.90	+.90	±0	−.52	−.33	+.08	+.08	+.60
20. Academic level of teaching																	+.91	+.33	+.40	−.67	−.14	−.14	−.14
21. Ability to teach																		+.76	+.76	+.76	+.76	+.85	−.20
23. Radicalism																			+.78	+.40	+.65	+.78	−.14
24. Level of aspiration own teaching																				+.78	+.65	−.14	−.14
26. Production of teaching material																					+.90	+.40	0
27. Interest in teaching																						+.60	+.20
28. Interest in theoretical items																							−.14
29. Years in department																							

are, however, general mechanisms, operating in the same way to create and enlarge differences between nations, universities, faculties and departments.

We admit that we did expect some differences between the two floors of the department; still, it was a surprise, and not a pleasant one, to find them so clear-cut and strong already at the micro level.

We now turn to the 83 teachers hired between 1958 and 1971 but not given tenure. As few of them had published anything, it was useless to study their research. We had to be content with some few data about their teaching. An assistant has estimated their research orientation on three scales, and so has a vice chairman which makes it possible to compute their reliability. We used seven variables:

1. Research orientation in 1972. 1. Empirical (neo-positivistic), 2. Theoretical (Marxist). Reliability +0.88.
2. Change toward theoretical orientation. 1. No, 2. Yes. Reliability +0.87.
3. Change toward empirical orientation. 1. No, 2. Yes. Reliability +0.70.
4. Has given courses in methodology. 1. No, 2. Yes.
5. Number of terms as teacher at the department. 1. 1–5, 2. 6 or more.
6. Academic degree. 1. B.A., 2. M.A. or Ph.D.
7. Still teaching at the department in spring 1973. 1. No, 2. Yes.

Four teachers had had so little contact with the department that neither the assistant, nor the vice chairman could estimate their research orientation. Our population, thus, was reduced to 79 teachers. They were hired by the chairman until in 1969, when the Board of the department took over the administration, which might mean that they gave more interest to the research orientation of the candidates. What is the relation between year of first employment and research orientation?

Research orientation	First employment at the department in							
	58–60	61–65	66–67	68	69	70	71	72
1. Empirical (neo-positivistic)	2	2	3	2	0	4	2	0
2. Theoretical (Marxist)	2	2	2	4	14	23	16	1

The chairman evidently hired just as many radical theorists as (more conservative) empiricists. The board preferred the radical theorists, but at this time most intelligent students tended to be radical. Anyhow, there is a decided change between 1968 and 1969. In 1972 only one teacher,

M.A., was hired, as the department had started to shrink; 44 teachers were fired in 1972 and 4 already in 1971. We relate this firing procedure to our other six variables, using the assistant's estimations of the first three ones. We present our data as correlations (Q-coefficients) in matrix 6, at the bottom of the page.

The matrix gives two clusters. The first is the radical cluster with a theoretical Marxist research orientation (variable 1) and a change in that direction during 1971–72 (2). The second cluster contains the remaining five variables: Change toward empiricism (3), teaching methodology (4), many terms as teacher (5), higher academic degree (6) and employment at the department in spring 1973. These two clusters are very clear-cut. All the ten correlations between the five variables in the second cluster are positive. Nine out of ten correlations between variables from different clusters are negative. One of these negative correlations, between variables 2 and 3, is, however, by definition −1. The only positive correlation between variables from different clusters (between 2 and 5) suggests that many old teachers changed their research orientation in the radical direction. If we apply the summation theory, we interpret the two clusters as an indication that the young teachers, anxious to be employed at the department, tried to use their radicalism to compensate their lack of empirical and methodological training, their few terms and lower degrees. The board of the department had, however, to pay attention to these two last merits. Radical teachers thus tended to be fired, but there is no indication, so far, that they have been either favored or maltreated.

Boalt had a hunch that radical teachers once they had been fired, tried to get employment in the survey research they previously had scorned. He suspected that they often presented a change of their research attitude toward empiricism.

Matrix 6. *Correlations from a sample of 79 teachers without tenure*

	1	2	3	4	5	6	7
1. Research orientation		+.78	−.50	−.15	−.30	−.66	−.37
2. Change toward theoretical orientation			−1	−.16	+.10	−.09	−.16
3. Change toward empirical orientation				+.59	+.17	+.31	+.27
4. Has given courses in methodology					+.38	+.46	+.10
5. Number of terms at the department						+.67	+.97
6. Academic degree							+.80
7. Still employed at the department							

The assistant's estimations do, however, not support this view. But the assistant has a radical orientation and would hardly appreciate a change in the empirical direction. The generation gap at the department is so deep, the communication between the generations so scanty, that it is neither difficult, nor dangerous to appear empirically oriented among the old generation and theoretically oriented among the young one. Our vice chairman belongs, however, to the old generation. If we compare his estimations with the assistant's we could easily sort out those teachers they estimate differently and see what happened to them. Were they fired or employed in 1973?

We start with differences in research orientation (variable 1) and present the data for the 16 cases in a table:

	Fired	Employed
More radical according to the vice chairman	3	6
More radical according to the assistant	0	7

Q-coefficient $+1$

There were only 3 fired teachers in this group, but all of them classified as radical by the vice chairman and as not as radical by the assistant.

We then turn to the differences in change toward theoretical orientation.

	Fired	Employed
Changed according to vice chairman, not acc. to assistant	4	1
Changed according to assistant, not acc. to vice chairman	9	4

Q-coefficient $+0.28$

There may be a tendency to employ those, who did not change in a radical direction according to the vice chairman.

Eventually we take up the change in opposite direction, toward empiricism:

	Fired	Employed
Changed according to vice chairman, not acc. to assistant	10	6
Changed according to assistant not acc to vice chairman	2	1

Q-coefficient -0.09

The correlation is very weak, only -0.09, but we expected a negative correlation, which would indicate that the employed after all had a tendency to give the vice chairman but not the assistant the impression that they had changed toward neo-positivism.

These three tables all point in the same direction: the generation gap is broad enough to protect the younger generation from the control of the older generation—as long as the youngsters do not publish and so unmask. Articles may escape the censorship but theses do not as they are marked by the professors. Youngsters with a traditional research ideology generally get on well, but radical researchers writing articles or theses have to make up their mind. Are they to pay lip-service to neo-positivistic research ideas or take the risk of low marks? This conflict creates frustration and does not stimulate radical research, thesis writing or publishing. Among our 79 junior teachers only 17 have, as far as we know, printed publications in sociology, generally articles in journals (reviews are not included). But radical sociologists tend to be younger and so tend to publish less. In order to reduce this effect we have divided the junior teachers in two groups: those who had taught less than 8 terms at the department and those who had more than 7. (We had to use this dividing line, as only 4 of the 17 had taught less than 6.) Two tables present the publication pattern in these two groups, but they are so similar, that we feel entitled to throw them together in a third table:

49 junior teachers, employed less than 8 terms, by research orientation and by publication in print

	Neo-positivists	Radicals
Junior teachers without printed publication	5	37
Junior teachers with printed publication	2	5
	Q-coefficient -0.49	

30 junior teachers, employed more than 7 terms, by research orientation and by publication in print

	Neo-positivists	Radicals
Junior teachers without printed publication	4	16
Junior teachers with printed publication	4	6
	Q-coefficient -0.45	

79 junior teachers, by research orientation and by publication in print

	Neo-positivists	Radicals
Junior teachers without printed publication	9	53
Junior teachers with printed publication	6	11
	Q-coefficient -0.52	

There is, as we expected, a marked tendency among radical junior teachers, independent of the time they have been employed at the department, to publish less than their neo-positivistic counterparts. This is hardly unknown to the professors, who tend to apply two interpretations. The first is that teachers, unable to publish, turn sour and attack the system, that has not rewarded their research. This interpretation may apply to teachers employed a long time but will not do for those hired recently. As both the categories show the same behavior we cannot accept this interpretation. The second is that the radical researchers neglect their duty, do not attend to their work properly. But this argument can just as well be used against the professors.

Accusations, frustration and aggression seem to be lavishly distributed to both sides of the generation gap. It is, after all, a heavy burden to a traditional and highly competent professor, eager to tell how research is to be done, that so many students, some of them very bright, turn a deaf ear to him. The generation gap then is a blessing. It serves as a protection against rudeness and painful confrontations, just as painful to both sides.

Gunnar Myrdal in *An American Dilemma* characterized the barrier between white and black in USA as the Glass wall. Special contact men were necessary to handle the interaction. Contact men are just as necessary at the sociological department to overcome the gap between traditional professors and young radical researchers. This task seems to have been taken over by the qualified assistant professors, who have made their Ph.D. with honors (docents). They are younger than the professors, more interested in theory, and they are comparatively independent of the professors. Some of them have the right to grade M.A. theses, but are allowed to grade Ph.D. theses only when temporarily acting as substitutes for full professors. They can, thus, hardly handle conflicts about Ph.D. theses. In the long run such conflicts will appear when radical theses are presented. There are three possible solutions. The professors may accept them, although the theses are not neo-positivistic. The professors may try to flunk them until the reaction is strong enough to make them yield. Or the radical researchers are slowly discouraged and eliminated, one at a time.

In our opinion the last solution is the worst. The lack of theory at the sociological department was a grave mistake. When the radical students stressed theory, for instance Marxist theory, this was accepted by several old teachers and stimulated their research. Theory is now respected at the department. Previously it was not. But the radical theorists not only have influenced several traditional sociologists, many of them have also themselves been influenced, are more willing to use empirical material. The neo-positivistic thesis has now met a Marxist anti-thesis and on both sides researchers have started to compromise, to work in the direction of synthesis.

Our discussion will seem strange to an American sociologist. University departments in the United States have many full professors, chosen so as to represent all the important theoretical and methodological approaches. The idea of large departments with one or just a couple of full professors forming a "school", that is, stressing the same theory, is alien to American universities. They do not understand, still less respect, the European idea of one professor—one department—one approach. American departments are anxious to present a "balanced curriculum" to the students and give them as free a choice of courses as possible. In our opinion this versatility of the university departments in the United States is one of the factors responsible for their high scientific standard. Swedish university departments are far more uniform. If there are several full professors at a department, representing different branches of the subject, they generally tend to share the same theoretical approach and direct their students in similar directions. This is in our opinion unfortunate, as "schools" of this kind tend to create barriers round themselves.

Radicalism is often by neo-positivistic sociologists viewed just as another "school", but if so it is international, in contact with other countries, other universities and other departments. In this study we are focusing our attention on barriers against communication. Radicalism then can be accused of creating generation gaps, but seems to do so especially in departments which have isolated themselves from other departments, other universities and other countries.

We have taken the full professors as representatives of the old generation. They occupy the top positions in the hierarchy of the department. They are no longer automatically chairmen of their department but still influential in the faculty, the research councils, the foundations, etc. The selection of full professors has then considerable consequences and we expect that the generation gap as well as the barriers between the departments will influence appointments of professors.

This procedure is complicated. First the chair has to be defined, then it is announced and the candidates apply for it, sending in their publications to prove their competence to the faculty. This faculty then selects three experts, full professors in the subject, and sends the publications to them in order to get the candidates ranked. After some months, when the experts are nearly ready, they meet at the university in order to listen to the candidates giving one or two academic lectures each, for the benefit of the experts, the faculty and members of the department. The experts have up to now worked independently, but now they discuss the candidates and their ranks. Some weeks later the experts send their reports to the faculty. If the three experts unanimously prefer the same candidate, he is always accepted by the faculty, which also tends to accept a candidate proposed by two of the experts. The faculty's proposal passes to the Chancellor of the Swedish Universities and from him to the government, which confirms the appointment. The first steps in this procedure can be influenced by local considerations and all of them by generation barriers.

Ulla Bergryd has studied the first and most important phase of this procedure and applied simple content analysis to the experts' reports. She found strong signs of barriers between departments, as no expert ever gave a candidate from his own department a lower rank (and very often a higher rank) than the other experts did. The generation gap is more difficult to elucidate, as the experts on the one hand sometimes dislike newfangled notions but on the other are anxious not to appear backward. Bergryd analyzed their comments on scientific innovations and found that these comments seemed to be used in a negative way, suggesting that the theory or method mentioned was bad but at least new. We could take that as a symptom, indicating that candidates too far off from the experts do run a risk to be underestimated.

The selection of professors probably has changed little, but the work they have to perform certainly has changed. A new professor still has to be the most qualified of the researchers applying for the chair, but formerly he was made chairman of his department and had to carry out so many administrative duties that he more or less gave up his own research. He had duties but he had also the security and power he had longed for while still subordinate to some other chairman. His research was important to him also as a vehicle of promotion. Once promoted he might try to build a new research empire, but more often he lost some interest in his own research. Instead his new role as chairman made it important to plan courses, change textbooks, select teachers and assistants, allocate research resources etc. But when the students late in 1968 began their drive against the academic Establishment, they no longer took value and purpose of teaching, textbooks and training for granted. The chairmen suddenly had to discuss and defend their decisions and goals. Most university departments were affected, especially in the social sciences, by the new ideology and the new generation conflict.

And so we turn for a moment our interest from the sociology department to the social science departments at the University of Stockholm.

We select spring 1967 as the last term before student unrest and compare the situation then with spring 1962 and with spring 1972. In 1962 there were eight social science departments and five years later seven of the eight chairmen still remained in this position. This demonstrates that professors in those days did remain chairmen. Only one of the chairmen had left, as he was promoted ambassador.

After 1967 teachers and students were anxious to take part in the administration of the departments and new regulations made it possible for them to do so. This did hardly suit the full professors, acting as chairmen. In spring 1967 there were ten social science departments, that is, ten chairmen. Five years later only one of them still held out; nine had had their fill of ideology conflicts and generation gaps. But how were then the new chairmen chosen? In the spring 1972 there were eleven departments with one chairman each. One of them was an old, experienced, full professor, six were full professors appointed after 1967 and four were assistant professors (docents), a category formerly only temporary chairmen (for short periods). In 1972 full professors evidently were little inclined to be chairmen and face generation gaps and ideology contrasts at every meeting. This seems to be true at least of the sociology department, where qualified assistant professors have taken the chairmanship in turn, thus probably reducing the generation gap a little.

This discussion has covered many fields. Let us review the main facts. Our study of *research patterns* have to be based on the M.A. theses, as most of the 67 researchers had published little else. All but twelve of them were written before 1967 and showed the traditional research pattern, where all research values were integrated into a single large cluster. The twelve last theses demonstrated, however, that although some young researchers still cherished traditional research values, they none the less paid little attention to methodology (formerly a central research value at Stockholm), to status from the professor and to contacts with him. Other researchers reacted in the opposite direction. We interpret this as a sign that good research at the department no longer is in touch with the professors of the department.

Looking at the teaching patterns, we can use a number of teaching traits on our 26 teachers, radicalism among them. We expected from the start that the 13 more radical and the 13 less radical teachers should overlap in many respects. The matrices demonstrated that they did, as the two matrices had much in common. The less radical teachers had a cluster of research values and a few teaching variables, 29, years at the department among them, but most of the teaching variables (1, 10, 21, 24, 26, 27 and, up to a point 28) formed a teaching cluster, indicating that traditional research values did not mix well with new, untraditional teaching. The radical teachers were better equipped to integrate traditional research values with radical teaching, as all research values and most teaching values formed one large cluster, the alternative cluster made up only of three values: 1) egostrength, 24) level of aspiration for teaching and 26) production of teaching material. (You must have egostrength and perform something if you feel accepted neither as a good researcher, nor as a good teacher).

We then divided the teachers according to the floor of their offices, this reduced the overlapping as the teaching pattern was perfectly integrated with the research pattern at the 8th floor, but badly integrated at the 9th, as this matrix fell apart in one research cluster and one teaching cluster.

So far we have covered the teachers with M.A. The moment we are interested in the staff policy, *the hiring and firing* of assistants, etc., we have to bring in the junior teachers without tenure at the department during 1971 and 1972. The chairman hired about as many neo-positivistic as radical teachers, but in 1969 the board of the department, dominated by radical students, took over this task and hired 54 radical versus 6 neo-positivistic teachers. The department began, however, to attract fewer students and the number of junior teachers had to be reduced. The board had to fire 48 teachers and this mainly hit the radical teachers with low degrees. Last hired, first fired.

Although several old teachers had, or got, a radical research orientation, we talk of a neo-positivistic older generation and a radical younger generation, trying to escape the control of the professors by creating a generation gap. This made it possible for some ambitious youngsters to join both sides, the radical dominating the teaching and the traditional one dominating research, as the professors mark theses, recommend grants, etc.

The generation gap at the sociological department may protect professors from radical critique but it also prevents them from attracting and training good students in traditional research technique. Ambitious professors regard this as an insult and react with frustration and aggression. But the radical young researchers do also suffer. Are they to accept rules they do not believe in and problems that do not interest them or are they to risk harsh critique and low marks? They too feel frustrated and their research suffers. We have demonstrated that the radical junior teachers have less often published in print than those who have a traditional research orientation. They tend to be frustrated in their research, the professors in their teaching.

There is, thus, a barrier against scientific communication within the department. Radical students are well aware of it, but until now they have not tried to enforce a passage: no radical theses have yet been presented. And what will happen then? Nobody can tell. But if they are acceptable and accepted, the barrier may be overcome. If they are not, the result may be a serious conflict. Or, the radical researchers may be silenced, outmanoeuvered, one after one, until only a few, frustrated diehards are left in a corner. If so, the department could once more rally round its colors, isolate itself from deviant international trends, from other departments at the university, now brought into contact by the radical researchers. From our point of view the radical researchers have taken part in creating a scientific communication barrier within the department, but they have succeeded in breaking its isolation, and that may be more important.

We now turn our attention to the selection of full professors among the candidates. Bergryd found a strong preference among the evaluating experts for candidates from their own department, a delightful kind of apostolic succession. Scientific innovation ought to be another important factor, but Bergryd found that this term generally was used in a negative sense, which might indicate that the experts prefer traditional research values in sociology. If so candidates for chairs had better not deviate from accepted sociological research patterns—until they have secured their appointment.

Then they can start building a research empire of their own. Most of them did not. Instead they started building an administrative empire. It was easier and more spectacular. They were chairmen of a department. They tried to expand the number of students, teachers, researchers, resources, grants, etc., using teaching, textbooks and even research reports for this purpose. This tendency to build administrative empires was strong before 1967 and much weaker afterwards, since chairmen in the social sciences not only, by new regulations, had to compromise with teachers and students but also to face generation conflict and ideological contrast. Full professors were no longer anxious to take care of departments too hot to handle. The chairmen accordingly often were selected among younger assistant professors.

Summing up some points: The sociology department seems to have got a generation gap concerning *research* recently. Conservative teachers

differ a little in *teaching* pattern from radical teachers, but these differences in teaching patterns are much stronger between the two floors in the department. The generation gap has created frustration and aggression among the older generation as well as among the young radical researchers, who suffer in their research. The conflict between the generations may culminate, if and when radical theses are presented. The generation gap does not visibly affect the selection of chairmen in the social science departments at Stockholm University. The sociology departments at Swedish universities have for many years built communication barriers between them, affecting citation patterns, and selection of full professors. The impact of radical research ideology may have created a generation gap, but radical researchers at the sociology department in Stockholm instead broke down the barriers against modern, international sociological theory and, against sociological research in the departments at Uppsala and Gothenburg.

Our description of communication and barriers in our own department can also serve as an illustration to Ben-David's critique of Kuhn (Joseph Ben-David: *The Scientist's Role in Society,* Englewood Cliffs 1971, pp. 3–6) as we have tried to show that "there may be (a) differences among individuals and groups in their perceptions of the breakdown (or exhaustion) of the paradigm due to either their different locations in the scientific community or differences in their individual sensitivity and (b) in the closure of certain scientific communities, that is, some may have nothing to do with other scientific communities, whereas others may have partially overlapping interests and common personnel. It is possible, therefore, to envisage normative variation leading to as fundamental a change as a revolution but issuing from the feelings of frustration and search for innovation of only a part of the scientific community".

Chapter 11

The communication of erroneous material, exemplified with nuclear family universality

Lewellyn Hendrix

With the publication of Murdock's (1949) assertions on the universal functions of the nuclear family, a conception of family structure was launched which was to have a great impact on the thinking of sociologists. In spite of a lack of precision in Murdock's definitions and a paucity of data in his presentation, his conception of the nuclear family as universal is widely believed to hold true with only rare exceptions. This paper will examine Murdock's definitions and data and will present some previously unnoticed contrary cases, leading to the question of why sociologists have accepted Murdock's formulation.

Murdock thought of the nuclear family as a concrete unit, existing independently or as the basic building block of more complex polygamous or extended family units. In his examination of 250 cultures, he concluded that regardless of what type of family structure prevails, the nuclear family is always visible as a functioning unit, performing important societal functions and fulfilling basic needs of its members. The nuclear family, as a specific type of unit, performs sexual, procreative, educational and economic functions. In Murdock's view these four functions of the nuclear family account for its universality, since it is doubtful that an adequate functional substitute for the family can be found (1949: 11).

In the debate following Murdock's publication, the contrary evidence presented has been anecdotal in form, centering on families in the Kibbutz (Spiro, 1954), the Nayar (Gough, 1959), and the traditional Chinese (Levy and Fallers, 1968). In the Kibutz and Nayar cases, the question has been raised as to whether a nuclear family exists. Among the tradi-

tional Chinese, however, there is some question as to whether the nuclear family is recognized as a functioning unit, separate from the extended family. Only Reiss (1965) has suggested that exceptions may be numerous, particularly among matrilineal North American Indians, and in the Caribbean area.

Murdock's formulation has been subject to criticism on conceptual grounds as well (Adams, 1960; Levy and Fallers, 1968; Reiss, 1965; Weigert and Thomas, 1971), but nevertheless it has had a definite impact on social theory, particularly in Parsons' (1964) work on incest taboos and Zelditch's (1955) study of nuclear family role differentiation. In both works, the conception of the nuclear family as a universally existing unit is a basic assumption.

In addition to its influence on theory, Murdock's formulation has entered into family textbooks. Recent family textbooks treating the issue of family universality typically give the impression that there are only one or two cases in which the nuclear family is not a concrete, functioning unit (Leslie, 1973; Bell and Vogel, 1968; Nye and Berardo, 1973; Schulz, 1972).

This acceptance in theory and in textbooks is somewhat puzzling in light of the lack of rigor in Murdock's definitions and the scanty evidence which he presents.[1]

Murdock's definitions

In an empirical work, one might expect to find clearly and precisely stated operational definitions. Such definitions are difficult to find in Murdock's work on the family.

The first problem with Murdock's definitions is that he does not define the family separately from its functions. The family is defined as "a social group characterized by common residence, economic cooperation and reproduction", including at least two opposite sex adults who "maintain a socially approved sexual relationship" established and defined by marriage customs, and one or more children (1949: 1). Included in this definition of the family are the economic, procreative, and sexual functions; only the educational function is not defined as an aspect of the family. Common residence, marriage customs and generation-sex structure are the only defining characteristics of the family not included in Murdock's list of functions.

Murdock's definition obscures the exact empirical question that he was trying to answer. On the one hand he may have been asking whether the nuclear family, as a residential unit with sexual, procreative, and economic functions, is universal. On the other hand, he may have been asking questions that seem more reasonable. One is the question of whether parents and children reside together in all societies, and the other is the question of what functions this unit performs in the societies in which it is found. Murdock's definition of family implies that he is examining the former question, while his discussion leans more toward the latter questions.

The definitions of the four nuclear family functions are more difficult to ascertain than is the definition of the family. The sexual function apparently refers to "the sexual privilege which all societies accord to married spouses" (Murdock, 1949: 4). Yet, Murdock states that "marriage exists only when the economic and sexual (functions) are united into one relationship", and marriage "forms the basis of the nuclear family" (1949: 8). In the latter statement, it is true *by definition* that the nuclear family has sexual functions. Why then did Murdock ask the *empirical* question of whether sexual intercourse is allowed between husband and wife?

The economic function consists of "economic cooperation, based upon a division of labor by sex" (1949: 7) and age within the nuclear family (1949: 8). The notion that economic cooperation occurs within the nuclear family, as opposed to some larger or differently composed kinship unit is particularly important, as will be seen in the discussion of Murdock's data below.

The procreative function is not specifically defined. It obviously refers to the birth of offspring in the nuclear family but also seems to refer to the regulation of abortion, infanticide, and neglect of infants and children (Murdock, 1949: 9). Were the procreative function to be defined solely in terms of childbirth, it would also be by definition a function of the nuclear family, which consists "of a married man and woman with their offspring" (Murdock, 1949: 1).

The educational function has to do with the acquisition of discipline and traditional knowledge and skill. Murdock states that "The burden of education and socialization everywhere falls primarily upon the nuclear family" (1949: 10), although outside agencies may assist. However, Murdock gives no indication of how he determined the range of variation of involvement of nuclear family personnel or of other agencies in the education of children. In Murdock's publication, no guidelines are pre-

sented for making the judgement that the nuclear family bears the burden of education.

In general, Murdock presents no clear and precise operational definitions of his concepts. The nuclear family was defined as having certain functions, and at the same time, Murdock attempted to examine the empirical question of whether the nuclear family performs these functions.

Murdock's data

Murdock's data were taken from the Human Relations Area File (initially called the Cross Cultural Survey). The data consist of categorized passages from published ethnographies and other descriptions of 250 "primitive" societies from all regions of the world. The Human Relations Area File (HRAF) was put together at Yale University, and at present, duplicate copies of it exist at over twenty universities, most of which are in the United States. Other microfilm copies are also in existence at various institutions. Over the years, additional materials have been coded and placed in HRAF.

There are several flaws in Murdock's presentation of his data. The two major ones are the lack of clear statements of the number of cases for which adequate information exists, and the presentation of irrelevant data.

In presenting his data, Murdock chiefly made statements to the effect that no exceptions to the assertions of universality were found. If, of course, the data are insufficient or missing for many societies, Murdock's generalizations would carry less weight. Unfortunately Murdock gives little indication of the number of cases for which adequate data exist, except to indicate that the data are inadequate to classify families as independent nuclear or complex in 23 percent of the cases (1949: 32). In other words, the maximum size of Murdock's working sample was 192 cultures rather than 250. In discussing the nuclear family functions no information whatsoever on missing data is given. One might speculate that the number of cultures for which Murdock had complete data is much less than 192.

Now let us look more closely at Murdock's style of data presentation. He states that no exception was found to the assertion that the nuclear family "exists as a distinct and strongly functional group in every known society" (1949: 2). Similarly, in discussing the sexual function, Murdock points out that it is:

genuinely astonishing that some society somewhere has not forbidden sexual access to married partners, confining them, for example, to economic cooperation . . . (1949: 4–5).

He then goes on to point out some near exceptions, and presents numerical data on the regulation of nonmarital and extramarital sex. Although interesting, this numerical data is not of direct relevance to Murdock's assertion on the sexual function of the nuclear family.

The only evidence presented on the economic function is a reference to Murdock's earlier paper on the division of labor by sex (1937). In this earlier paper, several tasks (e.g. hunting, herding, gathering of roots and tubers, water carrying, fuel gathering, fire tending, etc.) were coded according to the extent of male and female involvement in each. While the paper is important in that it shows that some tasks are almost always assigned to one sex or the other, it is irrelevant to Murdock's assertion on economic cooperation *within the nuclear family*. There is no way of telling from the evidence cited by Murdock whether the nuclear family, some larger kin group, or the community is a unit of cooperation or a base for dividing tasks.

In order to test the assertion on economic cooperation, one would need evidence on what tasks are performed by nuclear family personnel for the exclusive benefit of the nuclear family members. Murdock's data provides not even a clue as to whether there is economic cooperation within the nuclear family in this sense.

Of the remaining two functions, the procreative and educational, no specific data are presented (Murdock, 1949: 9–10). There are a series of generalizations about what must be done if society is to reproduce itself and about the implications of these necessities for the family unit. However, no evidence is brought to bear on these generalizations to show the reader that what must occur according to theory, is what actually does occur. Hence, it appears that sociologists have accepted Murdock's assertions more on faith than on facts.

A retest of Murdock's assertions

In view of the weaknesses in Murdock's presentation, an attempt was made to systematically retest his assertions, using HRAF materials. With the addition of materials over the years, the content of HRAF has changed somewhat, but much of the evidence examined was the same.

A set of operational definitions were developed in which the nuclear family was defined separately from its functions.[2] Using these definitions a data gathering instrument, similar to a questionnaire in format, was designed, with precoded response categories on all items. Several items on the instrument are combined to form a composite index for each of the five operational definitions.

The data were collected by undergraduate students in two sociology of the family courses in 1973. Prior to collecting the data, the students read and familiarized themselves with Murdock's assertions on the nuclear family. Each student was assigned three cultures from HRAF to examine, using the data gathering instrument and providing quotes from HRAF to document each item. This documentation was used to check and to improve the validity of the data.

During the period of data collection, some time was set aside during each class meeting to discuss problems of interpretation and coding. The coded data on the first culture examined by each student were compared by the instructor with the documentation. These data were returned to students with corrections and comments and were discussed in class. After the data collection was completed, students exchanged data sets and similarly checked one another's interpretation of the HRAF materials.

The data were then analyzed by the instructor and the findings were discussed in class.

A total of 213 cultures were examined, and 45 of these were examined twice in order to check on the reliability of interpretation of HRAF materials. Assuming that errors in each set of observations are equal, random, and independent, the average overall error rate on individual items is estimated to be 16 percent. In spite of these errors, the data are adequate to show some empirical weaknesses in Murdock's sample.

For a large proportion of the cultures examined, the information on the nuclear family and its functions was inadequate for classification or altogether absent (see table 1). Data on the sexual and educational functions were not to be found for about one-third of the cultures examined, while data on the procreative and economic functions were entirely absent on approximately one-half of the cultures. The data were present for only part of the items in each of the composite indices in one-fourth to four-fifths of the cases.

While highly specific meaning cannot be attached to the percentages in table 1 because of the errors present, the extent of missing or partially missing data appears to be great. We can assume that the amount of

Table 1. *Marginal distributions of composite indices of nuclear family characteristics*

Relation of data to assertion	Definition of family	Sexual function	Procreative function	Educational function	Economic function
Entirely missing	2%	33%	48%	36%	53%
Partial fit	33%	42%	24%	27% ⎫	
Entire fit	38%	19%	2%	19% ⎬	43%
Some contrary	27%	5%	26%	17%	4%
Total	213	213	213	213	213
Revised contrary[a]	9%	0%	0%	5%	1%

[a] These cases were selected from among those originally coded by students as contrary, after reexamination of documentation. Other cases, coded incorrectly, probably exist among the cases originally coded as not contrary.

information available to Murdock was somewhat similar to the distributions in the table. While some information in HRAF may have been overlooked in the present study, this bias is probably counteracted by the addition of materials to the files over the years. The implication is that Murdock's working sample was far fewer than 250 cases, and perhaps only half of that number. Thus, Murdock's assertions are in fact based on far fewer cases than they appear to be in his publication.

The documentation on cases originally coded as contrary was examined by the author to check for coding errors. For each of the functions and the definitions of the nuclear family, the proportion of contrary cases was revised downward, as can be seen in the last row of table 1. There may of course be other contrary cases among those originally coded as fitting Murdock's assertions or as missing data.

Seventeen cases are clearly indicated to be contrary to the definition of the nuclear family as a unit established by a marriage and having a common residence separate from that of other kin.

Seven cases were found in which it was stated that there is no ceremony or exchange by which a "marriage" is established. All of these cultures, nevertheless, appear to regard the relationship of a man and woman who reside together as socially acceptable, and distinguish it from other man–woman relationships.

In four more cases, including the renowned Nayar, the husband and wife have no common residence. Two of these cultures have men's houses, and in another, the husband, wife and prepubertal children of each sex reside in separate dwellings.

Two cases were found in which the nuclear family is not a residentially separate entity—the Jordanians and the Iban of Borneo. For Jordan, it is stated that two adult generations typically live in one room. The residential unity of the *bilek* family of the Iban is especially well documented. The Iban live in longhouses which are broken into apartments, each of which is occupied in the typical case by two generations of adults.

Four cases in which prepubertal children reside separately from parents were found. Children may live in dormitories as they do among the Gond from age six or seven, or with kin, as is the practice among the Thonga where children live with their grandparents for a protracted period after age three.

Initially, it appeared that several cases were contrary to the assertion on the sexual function, in that intra-family incest or marriage is allowed. For some of these cases, it became clear that father-daughter incest is only ritually practiced before hunts or before the marriage of the daughter. In other cases, such as the Vedda, it appears that some writers misinterpreted cross-cousin marriage as brother-sister marriage because of their failure to comprehend classificatory kinship terms. In other cases father-daughter or sibling incest seems to have occurred with some frequency although it is proscribed by norms. The Callinago and the Marshallese provide examples of this type of situation.

For one case, the Buka, the HRAF materials seem contradictory. Two authors reporting on this group agree that father-daughter incest occurs "not frequently". However, one report for the period 1895–97, states that father-daughter incest is not forbidden or considered a crime. A later report, for the period 1929–30, indicates that father-daughter incest is disapproved but not regarded with horror. Thus, it is impossible to tell whether incest norms have always existed in this group.

Twenty-six percent of the cultures originally were coded as contrary to the assertions on procreation. The operational definition of this function specifies that *norms* must regulate the practices of abortion, infanticide, and child neglect. After inspection, the data on none of these cases were sufficient to consider them contrary. In 18 cases, HRAF materials mentioned the frequency of such practices, without discussing the norms relating to them. In another 18 of these cultures, the materials spell out the circumstances under which abortion or infanticide are allowed. Common "extenuating circumstances" are illegitimacy and physical abnormality of offspring. In other cases, infanticide or abortion may be allowed when twins are born, births are closely spaced, many children have already been born in a family, or when there is an undesirable sex ratio among the offspring.

There are a few cases in which abortion, infanticide or neglect is of such magnitude as to suggest that these practices are not effectively regulated, especially the Nambicuara and the Malays among whom neglect is common, and the Crow, for whom it is said that two-thirds of the married women practice infanticide.

Although there are no cases in which abortion, infanticide and child neglect are clearly not normatively regulated, the data suggest that these practices have been common enough to influence the rate of natural increase of population in many tribal societies. This statement is, of course, contrary to the usual assumption of social scientists that natural death is the sole factor limiting the natural increase of population in these societies.

Twelve cases, among those originally listed, are contrary to the assertion that the nuclear family is the primary agent of education. Among some groups, such as the Ngoni, in which polygyny is the most common family form, the polygynous family rather than the nuclear family, appears to be the socializing agent. In other cases, grandparents or maternal uncles are very actively involved in socialization, as among the Thonga and Aleuts. In other cases, the HRAF materials indicate that children are placed under slaves, elderly widows, or kinsmen outside the immediate household for care and training. No case was found however in which no nuclear family personnel are involved. While some nuclear family personnel are always involved to some extent in education, it appears to be untrue both that these personnel always take care of the major part of the education of children, and that they universally act as a concrete unit in education.

In the original listing, eight cultures were coded as contrary to Murdock's assertion on economic cooperation in the nuclear family. Five of these were dismissed because adequate data were present for only one of the ten tasks in the operational definition. It would be misleading to cite these cases as contrary on such skimpy data. Another case, the Tallensi, was dismissed. Although all available data show economic cooperation of the polygynous family unit, the majority (60 percent) of the Tallensi families are monogamous. It is thus assumed that the monogamous nuclear family is typically a unit of cooperation.

Two cases, Albanian peasants and the Australian Tiwi, remain contrary to the hypothesis. The typical Tiwi residential family is polygynous, and nuclear units ordinarily cooperate with related units in food production (hunting and gathering) and consumption. The Albanian peasant situation differs in that a group of brothers or male cousins, along with their wives and children typically share a household, numbering 8 to 10 persons on the average in 1910. Although the nuclear family is a residential unit in that the husband and the wife share a bedroom in the joint household, there is no evidence that nuclear family personnel cooperate as a unit. Within the household, labor is divided within and between the sexes. The men split up the chores of herding, plowing and cutting hay, while the women divide the work of milking, collecting firewood, cooking and washing. All benefits are shared by all members of the household. Funds are put into a common purse, even when earned by one member working away from the household. Cooking for the entire joint household is usually done by one elder female.

Discussion

Murdock's work on nuclear family universality can be criticized *a priori* on the basis of lack of clarity in definition and data presentation. The data of the research presented in this paper, show clearly that there is a factual basis for criticism as well. Murdock may have had adequate data for only half of the 250 societies he examined. A total of 26 cultures in the present sample are contrary to Murdock's assertions in one way or another, and most of these have not previously been cited as contrary cases. Undoubtedly, more contrary cases exist for which the data were misinterpreted or overlooked during data collection. It must be concluded that the position of Reiss (1965) and Levy and Fallers (1968), that some small kinship unit or units exist in every society and participate to some extent in the socialization of children is a more adequate formulation than that of Murdock.

Specifically, the data suggest that all societies approve of some adult heterosexual relationships. It is neither true for all societies that some event (a marriage ceremony or exchange) marks the entrance into this relationship, nor that this sexual relationship involves a common residence of the couple and their immature offspring. Furthermore, the nuclear family unit is not always the major agent of socialization, and it is not always a unit of economic cooperation.

Given the empirical and conceptual weaknesses in Murdock's work on nuclear family universals, we may ask why his formulation has been so widely accepted.[3] We can however only suggest an answer which contains an element of speculation.

Perhaps the major factor explaining this acceptance has to do with the mood of sociology at the time Murdock published his work. Long before Murdock's publication, sociologists to some extent and anthropologists in particular had tried to develop a conceptual approach to the problem of variation in culture and social structure. During the nineteenth century, the unilineal evolutionary approach was at its height (C. F. Bachofen, 1861; Morgan, 1899; Engels, 1902). In this approach, cultural variation was understood as differences between the evolutionary stages which cultures have reached. Western society was perceived ethnocentrically in most evolutionary writings as being at the most advanced stage of development.

Aside from the ethnocentrism of the evolutionary approach, it had empirical difficulties. The correlation among cultural traits predicted by the evolutionists did not always occur (Murdock, 1937 b), and seeming anomalies were interpreted as "hold-overs" from previous stages. This type of interpretation led to a great deal of historical conjecture which was soon recognized as untestable for practical purposes since the cultural histories of non-literate societies could not be known with any accuracy.

There was a strong reaction to the ethnocentrism and fruitless conjecture of the evolutionary approach, which resulted in the establishment of the functionalist approach, which assumes that culture can be understood in terms of the interdependence of simultaneously existing elements.

In some versions of the functionalist approach, one particular cultural theme, such as the major value pattern, the descent rules, etc., is used to account for other elements in the cultural system.

The evolutionary approach was, until recently, almost completely abandoned. An example of this reaction is provided in Radcliff-Brown's (1924) criticism of Junod's earlier analysis of kinship in the BaThonga tribe of Africa. Junod had interpreted the nephew-mother's brother relationship in the patrilineal tribe as a hold-over from a previous matriarchal stage. Radcliff-Brown rejected the evolutionary interpretation and suggested that, the relationship with the mother's brother could be understood in terms of presently existing social arrangements.

It is a mistake to suppose that we can understand the institutions of society by studying them in isolation without regard to other institutions with which they coexist and with which they may be correlated . . . (1924: 17).

Thus, from the reaction to the evolutionary approach there developed the assumption that a culture can only be understood in terms of the simultaneously existing elements in it. Furthermore, a culture was to be *evaluated* only on its own terms, rather than in terms of its evolutionary development. This, of course, is the assumption of cultural relativism.

During the early part of the twentieth century, sociologists were made increasingly aware of cross-cultural variability through the writings of anthropologists such as Benedict (1934), Mead (1935), and Linton (1936). These cultural relativists tried to understand cultures in terms of the interdependence of co-existing elements, although Linton stressed cultural diffusion and "borrowing" of traits more than the others did.

It was during this time that interest in the area of culture and personality developed. The impact of culture on personality was well appreciated during this period, but the determinants of culture were less well understood. For example, Mead came to the conlusion during this period that:

". . . human nature is almost unbelievably malleable, responding accurately and contrastingly to contrasting cultural conditions" (Mead, 1935: 280).

At the same time, Mead provided no satisfactory explanation of these contrasts in cultural conditions. One is left with the impression that particular cultural patterns are determined by random historical occurrences. With such an inability to explain cultural variation, it is not surprizing that some sociologists began by midcentury to hunt for commonalities among the variations in cultural patterns.

The search for universals may have been spurred on by world events as well. Many sociologists and anthropologists, who might have espoused a doctrine of cultural relativism in the abstract, discovered difficulties when relativism was applied to Nazi Germany. The practices of the Nazis ran counter to the beliefs of the humanistic and liberal social scientists in America and in Europe. Moreover it became difficult to espouse an ideology that a culture could be understood and evaluated on its own terms when many social scientists and their students were about to embark on military careers to destroy the Nazis. The contradictions became too great for the doctrine of cultural relativism to continue unchallenged. This moral and ethical dilemma helps in understanding the search for universals and the positive reception given Murdock's assertions, which emphasized those elements that cultures have in common rather than stressing the ways in which cultures vary.

Thus, Murdock's assertions on nuclear family universality came at a time when sociologists were trying to come to grips with the enormous variation found in human societies. Murdock's notion of the nuclear family as the common denominator of family structure was the kind of idea that sociologists were looking for. It was a simple answer to the problems of cultural variation in general, and family variation, specifically.

Other factors facilitating the acceptance of Murdock's assertions were present in the field of family sociology itself. At the time of Murdock's publication and before, a social problems orientation prevailed in family sociology in America (Komarovsky and Waller, 1945). There was an emphasis on the importance of the family, and a preoccupation with the social problems of the family, which was seen by many as entering a state of decline with increasing urbanization and industrialization (cf., Burgess and Locke, 1945; Ogburn and Tibbits, 1934). There was little interest in theory construction, particularly at a general and comparative level (Christensen, 1954: 18). Research effort was concentrated almost exclusively on the urban American family. Many family sociologists were familiar with only the narrowest range of published ethnographies, and their awareness of cultural variation was for the most part limited to a small set of descriptions and typologies of family structure.

Murdock's explanation of the universality of the nuclear family on the basis of its necessity for human survival was one which fit in with the concern of sociologists with the importance of the family. Murdock's colleagues were, of course, familiar with the nuclear family as the type occurring in their own societies. It was a family type that they could readily understand and one which may have seemed "natural" to them as the basis of family structure everywhere. Few family sociologists would have been able to challenge Murdock, had they wanted to, because of their relative ignorance of the ethnographic data which Murdock had examined. Thus, being in no position to challenge Murdock's assertions, they could only accept them, at least tentatively, on faith. Since Murdock provided a simple way of dealing with the variation in family systems of which sociologists were aware, they were perhaps too eager to accept his notion that their own family type underlies all the variation in family systems. Thus, the handful of opponents of Murdock's view have kept the debate on nuclear family universals more or less alive for over two decades, but have had little success in reducing the widespread acceptance of Murdock's assertions.

References

Adams, Richard N., 1960. An inquiry into the nature of the family. In G. Dole and R. L. Caneiro (eds.), *Essays in the Science of Culture*, pp. 30–49. New York: Crowell.

Bachofen, J. J., 1861. *Das Mutterrecht*. Stuttgart.

Bell, Norman W. and Vogel, Ezra F., 1968. *A Modern Introduction to the Family*, New York: The Free Press.

Benedict, Ruth, 1934. *Patterns of Culture*. Boston: Houghton Mifflin.

Burgess, Ernest W. and Locke, Harvey J., 1945. *The Family: From Institution to Companionship*. New York: American Book Co.

Christensen, Harold T., 1964. Development of the family field of study. In H. T. Christensen (ed.), *Handbook of Marriage and the Family*, pp. 3–32. Chicago: Rand-McNally.

Engels, Frederick, 1902. *The Origin of the Family, Private Property, and the State*. Chicago: Kerr.

Geiger, H. Kent, 1968. The fate of the Family in Soviet Russia: 1917–1944. In N. W. Bell and E. F. Vogel (eds.), *A Modern Introduction to the Family*, pp. 48–67. New York: The Free Press.

Gough, Kathleen, 1968. Is the family universal? The Nayar case. In N. W. Bell and E. F. Vogel (eds.), *A Modern Introduction to the Family*, pp. 80–96. New York: The Free Press.

Komarovsky, Mirra and Waller, Willard, 1973. *The Family in Social Context*. New York: Oxford University Press.

Levy, Jr., Fallers, Marion J. and Fallers, Lloyd A., 1968. The family: Some comparative considerations. In Paul Bohannan and John Middleton, *Marriage, Family and Residence*, pp. 215–221. Garden City, N.J.: Natural History Press.

Leslie, Gerald R., 1973. *The Family in Social Context*. New York: Oxford University Press.

Linton, Ralph, 1936. *The Study of Man*. New York: Appleton-Century-Crofts.

Mead, Margaret, 1935. *Sex and Temperament in Three Primitive Societies*. New York: William Morrow.

Morgan, Lewis, 1877. *Ancient Society*. Chicago: Kerr.

Murdock, George Peter, 1937a. Comparative data on the division of labor by sex. *Social Forces* 15 (March): 551–3.

— 1937b. Correlations of patrilineal and matrilineal institutions. In G. P. Murdock (ed.), *Studies in the Science of Society*, pp. 445–470. New Haven: Yale University Press.

— 1949. *Social Structure*. New York: Macmillan.

— 1957. World Ethnographic Sample. *American Anthropologists* 20 (August): 664–87.

— 1967. *Ethnographic Atlas*. Pittsburgh, Pennsylvania: University of Pittsburgh.

Nye, F. Ivan and Berardo, Felix M., 1973. *The Family: Its Structure and Interaction*. New York: Macmillan.

Ogburn, William F. and Tibbitts, Clark, 1934. The family and its functions. In *Report of the Presidents Committee on Social Trend, Recent Social Trends in the United States*, pp. 661–708. New York: McGraw-Hill.

Parsons, Talcott, 1964. The incest taboo in relation to social structure and socialization of the child. In T. Parsons (ed.), *Social Structure and Personality*, pp. 57–77. New York: The Free Press of Glencoe.

Radcliff-Brown, A. R., 1924. The mother's brother in South Africa. Paper presented before the South African Association for the Advancement of Science, July 9, 1924. Reprinted in A. R. Radcliff-Brown (ed.), *Structure and Function in Primitive Society*, pp. 15–31. New York: The Free Press, 1965.

Reiss, Ira A., 1965. The universality of the family: A conceptual analysis. *Journal of Marriage and the Family* 27 (November): 443–453.

Schulz, David A., 1972. *The Changing Family: Its Function and Future*. Englewood Cliffs, N.J.: Prentice-Hall.

Spiro, Melford E., 1954. Is the family universal? *American Anthropologist* 56 (October): 839–846.

Wergert, Andrew J. and Thomas, Darwin L., 1971. Family as a conditional universal. *Journal of Marriage and the Family* 33 (February): 188–194.

Zelditch, Jr., Morris, 1955. Role differentiation in the nuclear family: A comparative study. In Talcott Parsons and Robert F. Bales (eds.), *Family, Socialization, and Interaction Process*, pp. 307–352. Glencoe, Ill.: The Free Press.

1 I do not mean to belittle Murdock's contribution to sociology in *Social Structure* or elsewhere. In spite of the shortcomings of the section in Social Structure on the nuclear family, I regard it as the most important book in the area of family and kinship studies. No other work approaches it in the breadth of theoretical issues treated and in the amount of data mustered in examining these issues. Murdock was a pioneer in comparative sociology and in addition to his many substantive and theoretical contributions has worked to compile data sets, such as The World Ethnographic Sample (1957), The Ethnographic Atlas (1967) and the Human Relations Area Files. These have facilitated the research of countless other researchers. Murdock's contribution is great indeed.

2 The following operational definitions were used in interpreting HRAF materials. The definitions specify the criteria which must be met if a case fits Murdock's assertions. The most commonly occurring patterns within a culture were used as the basis for classification

of a given case. Patterns applying only to minorities (e.g. nobility) were ignored in interpreting the data.

A. Nuclear family: (1) A man, a woman and their non-adult offspring have a *common* residence *separate* from that of nonmembers. (2) Some *ceremony* or *exchange* marks the entrance of man and woman into residential cohabitation.

B. Sexual function: (1) Sexual intercourse between husband and wife is allowed by the norms. (2) The norms do not allow sexual intercourse between other nuclear family members.

C. Procreative function: Norms regulate (but may in some cases not entirely forbid) abortion, infanticide and child neglect.

D. Educational function: (1) Nuclear family personnel primarily train and care for both male and female members during the first five years of life. (2) Nuclear family personnel primarily educate both male and female offspring until they reach puberty.

E. Economic function: From a list of ten tasks (from Murdock 1937) which benefit the prepubertal child, at least one is performed by nuclear family personnel.

3 I am especially indebted to Professor Herman R. Lantz for his insightful suggestions on the historical trends and events related to the acceptance of Murdock's work.